Kye Kim's
MODERN **KOREAN** COOKING

Kye Kim's
MODERN KOREAN COOKING

케 이   킴 의   모 던   한 국 요 리

BOOKHOUSE 북하우스

F O R E W O R D _Food from the Heart

I wanted to write this book for two reasons.

First, I wanted to teach my children how to cook both modern and traditional Korean food. The second reason is a personal desire to simplify the often complex recipes so that busy young professionals, 2nd generation Korean-Americans, and non-Koreans could easily make and enjoy Korean food at home.

I am often asked what makes my cooking different from other chefs'. I would have to say that I am not a chef, but a mother and wife who loves to cook for my family and friends. I would also have to add that I cook from the heart, and that my love for my family and cooking is well expressed through my food.

My daughter and I had a wonderful time writing this book together. When we began work on this book, she was a law student and extremely busy with her school work, but she set aside one day a week to help translate my work into English, taste-test, and check over each recipe. It gave us an opportunity to share ideas, work together, and create a book that exemplifies Korean food; a combination of both the modern and the traditional. I really want to thank her for the time we shared because I have so many beautiful memories to cherish in my heart.

Kye Kim

When my mother first suggested that we write this book together, I was hesitant. I do not consider myself a skilled cook, nor do I have any capacity to tell others how to cook. Growing up with a superb cook as a mother was not very conducive to learning the culinary arts. Despite her best efforts, I had absolutely no desire to cook anything myself as it was obvious that my mother could make any food more delicious than I could. Why eat my own poor cooking when I could eat gourmet food prepared by my mother? As I grew older and moved away from home, my mother could no longer cook my meals and the need for daily sustenance led to more exploration in the kitchen. I realized that I loved to cook and bake and my mother's daily lessons had taught me to develop a good palate. Now, I would consider myself "obsessed" with food and everything about it. Regardless of how much I love it, I have never tried to compare my cooking with that of my mother.

Growing up, I always hoped that some day my mother would use her great talents and share them with the world and this cookbook is a manifestation of that hope.

I wanted to do anything to encourage her and that is why I agreed to work on this book with her. I knew it would be a great opportunity to finally take advantage of those cooking lessons she has tried to offer so many times before, and to show her my support in her endeavors. As I said before, I may not be the most skilled of cooks but these recipes are accessible to someone like me and that is the central concept of this book. Most importantly, it gave me an opportunity to get to know my mother even better and we had a wonderful time together.

Michelle Kim

CONTENTS

PART 1 Appetizers & Entrees

PART 2 Soups & Salads

PART 3 Meat

PART 4 Seafood

PART 5 Rice & Noodles

PART 6 Kimchi

PART 7 Dessert

COOKING TIPS

It is important to remember that all of the recipes in this book are fluid and that many of the ingredients can be replaced according to whatever you have on hand. Thus, for something like rapini salad, there is no need to go through a huge effort to find rapini if it is not available. Something like broccoli would suffice just as well.

For instance:
1. Any vegetables in each dish can be replaced with other vegetables.
2. Any meat can be replaced or combined with other meat,
   such as replacing ground pork with ground beef. The same applies for seafoods.
3. If you do not prefer spicy foods, you can always tone down the amount of
   hot Korean chili sauce (red pepper paste) and replace with basic sauce or fish sauce.

01 Tips for using Korean spices

There are a few ingredients that every Korean cook should keep stocked in their kitchen:

1. Soy sauce
2. Sesame seed oil
3. Toasted sesame seeds
4. Garlic
5. Green onions
6. Ginger
7. Korean hot pepper paste (Gochujang)
8. Korean soybean paste (Doenjang)
9. Hot pepper powder (gochugaru)
10. Rice
11. Somen and Soba noodles
12. Tofu

02 Tips for grocery shopping

There are several easy ways you can live a more economical lifestyle
by changing the way you look at grocery shopping:

1. Buy meat on sale and cut into appropriate sizes for stews or other dishes
   and freeze for later use.
2. Make soup stock, such as chicken or beef stock, and freeze.
3. Bone-in chicken is often cheaper to buy and the bones can be used to make chicken stock.
4. Don't be afraid to go to more than one grocery store to get what you need at a good price.
5. It is very useful and economical to grow your own herbs and some vegetables,
   such as tomatoes, peppers, chives, parsley, mint, and spring mix lettuces.

03 Tips for using stocks

These are some things that will help create fast, easy, and delicious dishes without effort:

1. It is a good idea to season beef and beef stock and freeze them separately
   because they can be used to make several different dishes such as:
   - Mandu Guk: Boil the broth with some of the beef, add dumplings.
     You can also make Tteok Mandu Guk if you add Tteok.
   - Miyeok Guk: Soak wakame in water and add it to the beef and beef stock.
   - Yukgaejang: Boil broth with the beef, add hot pepper powder, green onion
     and other vegetables.
2. If you have chicken broth on hand you can make an easy noodle dish by boiling
   and adding Kalguksu noodles, shredded zucchini and green onion.
   - Chicken broth is also good for making Tteok Guk or Mandu Guk.
3. For many of the soups, you can replace the use of water with beef or chicken stock
   and improve the flavor immensely.

04 Tips for utilizing leftovers

Many of these dishes can be modified to create other dishes with minimal effort
and some ingredient substitution:

1. Gimbap can easily turn into California rolls by mixing Basic sauce into the hot rice
   instead of sesame oil and using avocado and crab meat as the filling.
   This is a simple twist on the traditional "inside-out" California roll.
2. Leftover coffee can be frozen and used to make Coffee Bingsu.
3. You can add matcha(nokcha powder), orange zest, cocoa powder, or butternut squash puree
   to the batter to make different flavors of Maejakgwa.
4. If you have leftover Samgyetang, you can use the leftover broth and meat
   to make Dakjuk by adding some leftover rice and boiling it.
5. If you have leftover Jeon and some beef broth, you can easily use both
   to make Sinseollo or Dubu Jeongol.
6. Ssamjang can be combined with fresh vegetables and rice to make an easy Bibimbap.

05 Tips for cooking noodles

When you boil noodles, add about 1/2 of a cup of cold water in the middle of the boiling process
in order to improve texture and taste and then bring water back up to temperature to continue
the boiling process. After the noodles are done, drain and rinse with cold water.

06 Tips for using the freezer

Many people do not utilize their freezers well to save time and money. However, it is one of the most important tools you can use to help live a more economical lifestyle, for instance:

1. To save time, Bingsu can be made ahead in single servings and kept in the freezer and taken out when you are ready to eat.
2. Gotgam Ssam can be made ahead of time and wrapped in plastic wrap and placed in the freezer. When you are ready to prepare, just thaw out the meat and slice.
3. Chestnut season is very short and are hard to find. When in season, you can roast, peel, and freeze for later use.
4. Drinks such as Sikhye and Sujeonggwa can be time consuming to prepare. Both can be made in advance and frozen. You can defrost and drink at a later time.
5. As stated in the grocery shopping tips, you can buy meat when it is on sale, marinate it, and freeze it for later use.
6. Freeze chicken and beef broth for later use.
7. Mincing garlic can be very time consuming, but if you have some free time, preparing a lot of garlic, dividing into small portions, and freezing it for later use can be a good time saver.
8. The easiest way to make ginger juice is either to grate fresh ginger and squeeze out the juices or to freeze chunks of ginger, defrost in the microwave, and squeeze. About 1 inch of ginger root makes about 1 tablespoon of ginger juice.

07 Tips for substitutions of cooking tools

One of the main purposes of this book is to make Korean food accessible to 2nd generation Koreans and non-Koreans. Many hard-to-find Korean kitchen utensils can be replaced with tools found in most kitchens, such as:

1. For Albap dishes, if you do not have a hot pot, you can marinate rice with sesame oil and salt and heat it in the microwave. Place the other ingredients on top to simulate the heat from the hot pot.
2. Rice can be prepared in a regular saucepan if you do not have an electric rice cooker but cleaning can be a bit difficult, so investing in a small, inexpensive electric rice cooker may be more convenient in the end.
3. For Sinseollo, you can use a dutch oven instead of a hot pot or Sinseollo pot.

08 Tips for stir frying

1. The cooking time for each ingredient is different, so you should stir fry each ingredient separately in order to preserve texture and avoid overcooking or undercooking.
2. Be careful not to overcook seafood as it can become rubbery and unpleasant to eat.

- 요리법에 나온 재료를 모두 갖춰야 할 필요는 없습니다. 당장 집에 있는 재료부터 사용해보세요. 예를 들면 레피니 겉절이를 하는데 레피니가 없다면 브로콜리로 대신해도 되고, 쇠고기는 돼지고기로 대신하고요. 이처럼 야채는 야채끼리, 고기는 고기끼리, 해물은 해물끼리 서로 바꿔 사용할 수 있답니다. 매운 음식이 싫은 분들은 고춧가루나 고추장을 덜 넣거나, 대신 베이직소스나 피시소스를 사용하셔도 좋습니다.

- 한국 부엌이라면 꼭 갖춰야 할 기본재료들이 있지요. 간장, 참기름, 볶은 깨, 마늘, 파, 생강, 고추장, 된장, 고춧가루, 쌀, 소면국수, 메밀국수, 두부를 늘 갖춰 놓는다면 언제나 안심이지요.

- 장보는 방법을 조금만 바꿔도 식비가 절약된다는 사실을 아세요? 첫째, 세일 중인 고기를 큰 덩어리로 사서 스튜 등 각각의 요리에 알맞은 크기로 썰어 냉동보관하거나, 쇠고기나 닭고기 육수를 대량으로 내서 필요한 분량만큼 나누어 냉동보관하세요. 필요할 때마다 꺼내서 녹여 쓰면 돈도 절약되고 간편해 일석이조랍니다. 둘째, 뼈를 바르지 않은 닭고기는 살코기보다 저렴하고 국물맛을 더 좋게 한답니다. 셋째, 똑같은 재료를 더 싸게 살 수 있다면 마트를 한두 군데 더 들르는 발품쯤은 필수지요. 마지막으로 토마토, 고추, 상추 등의 야채나 차이브, 파슬리, 민트 같은 향신초는 집에서 길러 드시면 어떨까요?

- 쇠고기나 닭고기 육수는 미리 양념해서 냉동고에 상비해두면 맛있는 요리를 언제든지 신속하게 만들어낼 수 있습니다. 쇠고기 육수는 (떡)만둣국, 미역국, 육개장 요리에, 닭고기 육수는 칼국수에 쓰면 어울리지만, 떡국이나 (떡)만둣국에 쓰셔도 좋습니다. 다른 국을 만들 때도 물 대신 쇠고기나 닭고기 육수를 해동해 쓰시면 더 좋은 맛을 낼 수 있지요.

- 재료를 조금만 바꿔 주는 수고만으로도 전혀 색다른 요리로의 변신이 가능하답니다. 첫째, 김밥을 만들 때 참기름 대신 베이직소스로 밥에 간을 하고 김밥소로 아보카도와 게맛살을 넣어주면 '옷 입은' 캘리포니아롤이 되지요. 둘째, 원두커피를 끓이고 남은 것을 얼려 두었다가 커피빙수를 만들 때 사용해보세요. 셋째, 녹차, 오렌지 제스트, 코코아 가루, 단호박 등을 매작과 반죽에 더해보세요. 색다른 매작과 향을 느낄 수 있답니다. 넷째, 삼계탕 남은 것이 있다면 찬밥을 넣어 닭죽을 끓여보세요. 다섯째, 쓰고 남은 갖가지 전들은 쇠고기 육수에 넣어 끓여 신선로나 두부전골을 만들 수 있습니다. 마지막으로 신선한 야채와 밥에 고추장 대신 쌈장을 넣어 비비면 몸에 좋은 비빔밥이 쉽게 완성됩니다.

- 마른국수는 끓는 중간쯤 물 반 컵을 부어서 더 끓이면 쫄깃하고 맛있게 삶아집니다. 다 삶아진 국수는 찬물에 넣어 씻어주세요.

- 냉동고를 지혜롭게 이용한다면 시간을 절약할 수 있습니다. 첫째, 빙수를 미리 만들어 냉동고에 넣었다가 후식으로 내보세요. 둘째, 미리 만들어 놓은 곶감쌈을 랩에 싸서 얼렸다가 필요할 때 꺼내서 녹인 후 썰어 내면 좋습니다. 셋째, 제철에 나왔다가 금방 들어가 버리는 밤은 한꺼번에 많이 사서 오븐에 구운 후 껍질을 벗겨 얼려놓았다가 녹여 씁니다. 넷째, 준비하는 데 시간이 많이 드는 식혜나 수정과도 미리 만들어 얼려놓으면 손님대접에 유용하게 쓰입니다. 다섯째, 세일 중인 고기를 큰 덩어리로 사서 미리 간을 한 다음 필요한 분량만큼 나누어 냉동보관하세요. 여섯째, 쇠고기나 닭고기 육수를 내서 얼려놓았다가 써보세요. 마지막으로 마늘을 한꺼번에 다져서 작은 덩어리로 나눠 냉동보관하면 언제나 꺼내 쓸 수 있습니다.

- 한인 2세나 외국인들이 찾는 데 어려움을 겪곤 하는 한국 조리기구는 다음과 같이 대체할 수 있습니다. 첫째, 뚝배기 대신 전자레인지를 이용해서 알밥을 만들어보세요. 소금과 참기름으로 간을 한 밥을 전자레인지에 넣고 데운 후 꺼내어 다른 재료들을 얹어 비벼먹으면 됩니다. 둘째, 전기밥솥 대신 일반 소스팬에 밥을 할 수 있지만 설거지가 힘이 들지요. 작은 사이즈의 저렴한 전기밥솥을 구입하는 게 더 편리할 거예요. 셋째, 신선로나 뚝배기를 사용하는 요리에는 더치 오븐을 사용해보세요.

- 스터프라이(볶기) 할 때, 각각의 요리재료를 따로따로 볶는 게 좋습니다. 재료마다 익는 시간이 다르므로 따로 볶아야 알맞게 익고 씹는 맛이 살아 있게 됩니다. 해물요리는 오래 익히면 질겨지고 식감이 나빠지므로 조심해야 합니다.

- 대부분은 생강을 강판에 갈거나 손으로 짜서 강즙을 내지만, 냉동된 생강을 전자레인지에 녹여서 손으로 짜는 방법이 제일 쉽답니다. 보통 생강뿌리 1인치에서는 1큰술의 즙이 나옵니다.

Appetizers & Entrees

chilled noodle and
shrimp lettuce wraps 국수냉채쌈 Guksu Naengchae Ssam

Nangchae is a fresh salad that is best served on hot summer days. The literal meaning of Nangchae is chilled vegetables. My mother makes this salad when she has guests over for dinner. One day when preparing this for a few friends, she realized that if noodles are added, it would make a great meal instead of an appetizer. She changed the dressing, and decided to put noodles, shrimp, and fresh vegetables in lettuce cups to make a refreshing lettuce wrap.

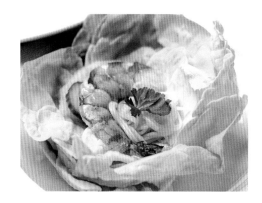

• 5 fresh large shrimp • 1 bundle somen noodles

• 1/2 Asian pear, peeled and cut into thin rectangle slices

• 2 pickling cucumbers or baby English cucumbers,
  cut into thin rectangle slices

• 10 lettuce leaves, washed and dried

• Parsley for garnish (optional)

Vinegar soy dressing

• 1 tbsp soy sauce

• 1 tbsp Basic sauce
  (Basic sauce is made 5 parts vinegar to 4 parts sugar to 1 part salt)

• 1 tsp oyster sauce • 1 tbsp olive oil • 1 tbsp lemon juice • 1 tsp sesame oil

Mix all ingredients for vinegar soy dressing and set aside.

Wash shrimp, leaving shells on and carefully cut down the backbone and remove vein. Cook shrimp in boiling water until they turn pink and are cooked through. Drain and set aside to cool. Peel and cut each shrimp in half, lengthwise. Cook somen noodles according to the directions on the package and rinse with cold water. Drain well and make small bundles. Arrange shrimp, cucumber, pear, and somen noodles on lettuce and pour dressing over them to taste. Garnish with parsley and serve.

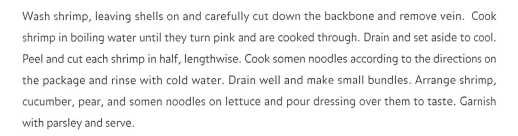

• 큰 새우 5개 • 소면 1인분 • 배 1/2개, 껍질을 벗기고 길이로 얇게 썬다. • 오이 1개, 5cm 길이로 잘라 얇게 썬다. • 양상추 또는 작은 상추 10장 • 파슬리 조금(장식용) 초간장 드레싱 • 간장 1큰술 • 베이직소스 1큰술 (식초 5 : 설탕 4: 소금 1) • 굴소스 1큰술 • 올리브유 1큰술 • 레몬주스 1큰술 • 참기름 1작은술 초간장 재료를 잘 섞어둔다.

새우를 껍질째 등을 갈라 내장을 빼고 잘 씻어둔다. 새우가 핑크색으로 변할 때까지 끓는 물에 삶고 나서 찬물에 담가 식힌다. 새우껍질을 까고 길게 반으로 자른다. 소면을 삶아 찬물에 헹군 후, 한입 크기로 말아 물기를 빼놓는다. 상추 위에 국수를 놓고 썰어놓은 새우, 오이, 배를 예쁘게 담아 파슬리로 장식하여 접시에 담고 준비해둔 드레싱을 끼얹어낸다.

stuffed kimchi
with tofu and pork 김치두부고기쌈 Kimchi Dubu Gogi Ssam

My mother created this recipe as a way to entice me into incorporating more tofu into my diet. I used to complain that it was too hard to figure out how to cook tofu in flavorful ways except adding it to a soup. She knows that I absolutely love ssam, which typically consists of wrapping different fillings into delicious bundles of different flavors and textures. So, she developed Kimchi Dubu Gogi Ssam. After tasting this recipe, I haven't had any problems eating more tofu.

- 1 whole napa cabbage, made into kimchi • 1/2 lb pork loin, sliced thin
- 1/2 lb firm tofu • 1 tbsp brown sugar • 1 tbsp water • Vegetable oil • 1/4 tsp salt

Marinade for pork

- 1 tbsp soy sauce • 1 tsp chopped green onion • 1/2 tsp minced garlic
- 1 tsp toasted sesame seeds • 1 tbsp sesame oil • 1/8 tsp black pepper

Mix together all the ingredients for the marinade except sesame oil and set aside. Stir together brown sugar and water until sugar is mostly dissolved. Pour sugar water mixture over the meat and mix until meat is well coated. Let sit for about 5 minutes. Pour prepared marinade over the meat and mix until it is well coated. Then add sesame oil and mix again to coat.

Cook meat in a large frying pan and set aside. Slice the tofu into long pieces about 1 inch tall, 1 inch thick, 3 inches long. Sprinkle lightly with salt. Heat a tablespoon of vegetable oil in a large frying pan and cook each tofu piece until the sides are light golden brown. Spread the kimchi leaves flat and then place cooked pork on top and then place fried tofu in the middle. Roll the kimchi leaves and fillings into a log and slice into 1 inch pieces.

• 김치 1포기 • 돼지고기 450g(얇게 썬 것) • 단단한 두부 1/2모 • 흑설탕 1큰술 • 물 1큰술 • 식용유 조금 • 소금 1/4작은술 **돼지고기 양념장** • 간장 1큰술 • 다진 파 1작은술 • 다진 마늘 1/2작은술 • 볶은 깨 1작은술 • 참기름 1큰술 • 후추 1/8작은술 **참기름을 뺀 돼지고기 양념장** 재료를 잘 섞어 옆에 둔다.

흑설탕을 녹인 물을 썰어놓은 돼지고기에 부어 5분간 재어둔다. 준비한 양념장을 고기에 넣어 버무린 후 참기름을 넣어 재어둔다. 뜨거워진 프라이팬에 고기를 펴서 익힌다. 두부를 가로세로 2.5cm 길이 7cm로 썰어, 소금을 살짝 뿌려 달군 프라이팬에 지져낸다. 익힌 돼지고기를 펼친 김치 위에 놓고 두부를 가운데 놓아 돌돌 만 다음 먹기 좋은 크기로 자른다.

pancake rolls 밀쌈 Milssam

Milssam is a simplified version of Gujeolpan, which refers to an elaborate Korean dish consisting of nine different foods assorted on a wooden plate. It is less formal and makes a great canape when wrapped into individual portions.

- 1 cup flour • 1 cup water • 1/2 tsp salt
- 1/2 carrot, peeled and minced, squeeze juice in separate bowl to use for yellow pancakes
- 1/2 cucumber, outer skin only, minced, squeeze juice in separate bowl
  to use for green pancakes
- 1/3 lb chicken breast, thinly sliced into long pieces and marinated
- 1/2 green bell pepper, thinly sliced into long pieces
- 1/2 red bell pepper, thinly sliced into long pieces
- 1 large sheet red cabbage, thinly sliced into long pieces

Marinade for chicken

- 1 tsp mirin • 1/4 tsp salt • 1 tsp sesame oil

Dipping sauce

- 1 tbsp soy sauce • 1/2 tbsp sugar • 1/2 tbsp vinegar
- 1 tsp prepared Asian hot mustard (optional)

Mix all the ingredients for the dipping sauce in a bowl and set aside.

Make Pancakes

Mix together the flour and water in a tall glass cup and leave covered in the refrigerator overnight.

Note

This step is not absolutely necessary but improves the texture of the pancakes immensely. The flour and water should separate with the water floating on top of the flour. Pour out and discard the water. Separate the flour into three small bowls and mix with the carrot juice in one bowl and the cucumber juice into another. Add a pinch of salt to all three bowls and mix together.

Heat a large skillet over medium heat and add about 1 teaspoon of vegetable oil. Using a dry paper towel, wipe up excess oil to make sure that the skillet is evenly coated. When it is hot, carefully put about 1 tablespoon of batter into the pan, spreading it outward with the back of a spoon until it makes a circle about 4 inches in diameter. When the surface of the pancake facing upward appears dry, flip the pancake over and cook the other side. Remove the cooked pancake before it begins to brown. Continue making pancakes until the batter in all the bowls is used, laying the finished pancakes on a paper towel to drain. Refresh the pan with oil when needed.

Make Fillings

Quickly sauté the green pepper for a few seconds in a hot skillet with a little bit of vegetable oil and a pinch of salt. Repeat the same process with the red pepper and red cabbage. You will be sautéing the marinated chicken breast as well, but with sesame oil instead of vegetable oil. Sauté the chicken in the same manner as the other ingredients. Keep each filling separate and set aside.

Place a little of the chicken and vegetables onto the center of a pancake and roll tightly.
Serve at room temperature with the dipping sauce.

• 밀가루 1컵 • 물 1컵 • 소금 1/2작은술 • 당근 1/2개, 갈아 즙을 짜둔다. • 오이 1/2개, 껍질을 벗겨 즙을 짜둔다. • 닭가슴살 300g, 가늘게 채썰기하여 밑간양념에 재어둔다. • 피망 1/2개, 가늘게 채 썬다. • 홍피망 1/2개, 가늘게 채 썬다. • 적양배춧잎 1장, 가늘게 채 썬다. 닭가슴살 밑간 양념 • 맛술 1작은술 • 소금 1/4작은술 • 참기름 1작은술 소스 • 간장 1큰술 • 설탕 1/2큰술 • 식초 1/2큰술 • 갠 겨자 1작은술 소스재료를 잘 섞어둔다.

밀전병 만들기 밀가루 1컵에 물 1컵을 넣어 잘 섞어 냉장고에 하룻밤 놓아둔다. 가라앉은 밀가루 앙금이 보이면 위의 물을 따라버리고 소금을 넣어 잘 섞은 후 3등분하여 각각 다른 그릇에 넣고 한 개의 그릇에는 당근즙을, 다른 그릇에는 오이즙을 섞어둔다. 팬을 달군 후, 종이타월에 기름을 묻혀 팬에 골고루 바른다. 풀어놓은 밀가루를 한 순가락씩 덜어 동그랗고 얇게 전병을 부쳐 색색의 전병을 만들어둔다. 속재료 만들기 달군 팬에 기름을 두르고 중불에 썰어놓은 재료들을 각각 따로 볶아낸다. (같은 팬을 쓸 경우에는 재료가 바뀔 때마다 팬을 키친타월로 닦아 사용한다.) 부쳐놓은 밀전병 위에 볶아둔 속재료를 조금씩 넣어 돌돌 말아 예쁘게 접시에 담고 소스와 함께 낸다.

spicy tofu meat sauce

두부고기쌈장 Dubu Gogi Ssamjang

This meat sauce is the item in my mother's repertoire that I missed most when I left for college, and was the first recipe I asked for when we began to prepare for this book. I love the combination of the Korean Miso(fermented soybean paste called doenjang) combined with bits of ground pork and the spiciness of the Korean hot pepper paste(gochujang). I used to pile this sauce on top of rice as a make-shift dinner, but I love it best wrapped in cool bundles of lettuce with warm rice.

- 1/2 lb ground pork • 1/2 medium size onion, chopped
- 1/2 lb hard tofu, smushed into small chunks • 1 tsp ginger juice
- 1+1/2 tbsp gochujang (Korean hot pepper paste)
- 1+1/2 tbsp doenjang (Korean soybean paste) • 1 tbsp sugar • 1 tbsp cooking wine
- 1 tsp minced garlic • 2 tbsp chopped green onion • 1 tbsp sesame seed
- 2 tbsp sesame oil • 2 tbsp water

Gochujang sauce

- 2 tbsp gochujang • 1 tbsp vinegar • 1 tbsp sugar • 1 tsp toasted sesame seeds
- 1/2 tsp minced garlic • 1/2 tsp chopped green onion • 1 tsp sesame oil

Mix together all ingredients and use as an additional dipping sauce for the vegetables.

Place sesame oil in a large frying pan over medium heat and add chopped onion and pork. Pour ginger juice over the mixture and sauté until pork is fully cooked and onion is softened. Add all of the rest of the ingredients and mix together. Cook for a few more minutes to allow ingredients to combine. Serve as a dipping sauce for vegetables.

If you wish, you can also serve with gochujang sauce as an additional dipping sauce.

• 간 돼지고기 450g • 양파(중) 1/2개, 다진다. • 두부 1/2모, 잘게 으깬다. • 생강즙 1작은술 • 고추장 1+1/2큰술 • 된장 1+1/2큰술 • 설탕 1큰술 • 맛술 1큰술 • 다진 마늘 1작은술 • 다진 파 2큰술 • 볶은 깨 1큰술 • 참기름 2큰술 • 물 2큰술 고추장소스 재료 • 고추장 2큰술 • 식초 1큰술 • 설탕 1큰술 • 볶은 깨 1작은술 • 다진 파 1/2작은술 • 다진 마늘 1/2작은술 • 참기름 1작은술 고추장소스 재료를 잘 섞어 원하는 생 야채와 함께 낸다.

프라이팬을 중불로 달군 후 참기름을 두르고 다진 양파, 고기와 생강즙을 넣고 익을 때까지 볶은 다음, 나머지 재료를 다 같이 넣고 잘 섞어 몇 분간 더 볶는다. 원하는 쌈야채와 같이 곁들여낸다.

steamed squid with vinegar-chili sauce

오징어초회 Ojingeo Chohoe

When I was little I was completely obsessed with the chewy texture of the squid served with vinegar-chili sauce. I would get a plate of squid, sit down at the kitchen table, and slowly bite into the springy, tender squid. I was so fascinated by the way my teeth would bounce off of the surface of the smooth, white squid, yet immediately slice cleanly through until a small chewy piece was left on my tongue. This dish makes a great midnight snack and is a fresh alternative to stir-fried squid.

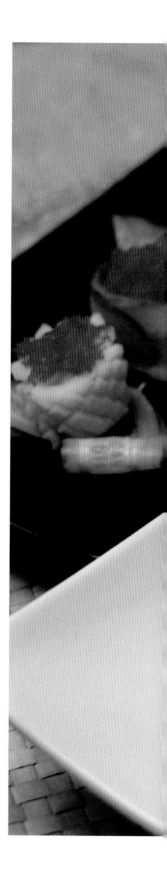

- 1 large squid tube (body only), cut open and cleaned
- 2 tbsp flying fish eggs

Dipping sauce
- 2 tbsp Korean hot pepper paste (gochujang) • 1 tbsp sugar
- 2 tbsp vinegar • 1 tsp minced garlic • 1 tbsp chopped green onion
- 1 tsp toasted sesame seeds • 1 tbsp sesame oil

Mix all ingredients for sauce and set aside.

Using the tip of a knife, score the side of the squid that curls inward in a crisscross pattern. Bring a large pot of water to a boil. Add squid and cook until it just starts to curl, about 3 minutes. Drain and slice into 1 inch round pieces. Arrange the squid on a thin slice of cucumber with flying fish eggs on top or wrap a thin slice of cucumber around each piece.

Serve the squid with the vinegar-chili sauce (vinegar hot pepper paste).

• 오징어(몸통) 1마리 • 날치알 2큰술 • 오이 1개, 길이로 얇게 썬다. 초고추장 • 고추장 2큰술 • 설탕 1큰술 • 식초 2큰술 • 다진 마늘 1작은술 • 다진 파 1큰술 • 볶은 깨 1작은술 • 참기름 1큰술 초고추장 소스 재료를 잘 섞어둔다.

오징어 몸통을 깨끗이 씻어 껍질을 벗기고 안쪽에 가로세로 칼집을 넣은 후 한입 크기로 잘라 끓는 물에 살짝 데쳐 한입 크기로 잘라 둔다. 얇게 썬 오이 위에 오징어를 놓고 날치알을 올린 다음 접시에 예쁘게 담아 초고추장과 함께 낸다.

Korean dumplings

편수 Pyeonsu

There are many kinds of Korean dumplings, all of which are grouped under the universal category of Mandu. This particular kind is called Pyeonsu because of its unique shape. My mother is very passionate about the idea that food must be aesthetically pleasing as well as delicious, and Pyeonsu satisfies both those requirements. Unlike more "normal" types of Mandu, the addition of pine nuts and bits of egg elevate the dumplings to another level.

- 1 package square dumpling skin • 1/4 lb ground beef • 1/4 lb ground pork
- 1/2 lb of medium or hard tofu
- 2 dried shitake mushrooms, soaked in the warm water to reconstitute
  for 30 minutes and chopped
- 1 zucchini, shredded and sprinkled with salt

- 1 egg, made into a thin omelet and cut 1/2 inch diamond shapes
- 2 tbsp pine nuts • 1 egg white

Seasoning
- 1 tsp soy sauce • 1/4 tsp salt • 1 tsp minced garlic • 1 tbsp chopped green onion
- 1 tsp toasted sesame seeds • 1 tbsp sesame oil • 1/8 tsp black pepper • 1 tsp ginger juice

Dipping sauce
- 1 tbsp soy sauce • 1/2 tbsp sugar • 1/2 tbsp vinegar

Mix together all ingredients for dipping sauce and set aside.

Squeeze the water from the bean curd and zucchini. Add the seasonings to all the ingredients except the egg and pine nuts. Place the mixture with 1 egg slice and 2 pine nuts on the each square. Brush around square with egg white or water. Pinch the four edges together tightly to make a square shaped dumpling. Repeat with the rest of the ingredients until you have used up all of the filling and dumpling skins. Steam or boil and serve with dipping sauce.

• 네모만두피 1팩 • 간 쇠고기 150g • 간 돼지고기 150g • 두부 1/2모 • 마른 표고버섯 2개, 불려 다져놓는다. • 호박 1개, 채 썰어 소금을 뿌려둔다. • 달걀 1개, 지단을 부쳐 마름모꼴로 썰어둔다. • 잣 2큰술 • 달걀 흰자 1개 양념 • 간장 1작은술 • 소금 1/4작은술 • 다진 마늘 1 작은술 • 다진 파 1큰술 • 볶은 깨 1작은술 • 참기름 1큰술 • 후추 1/8작은술 • 생강즙 1작은술 초간장 • 간장 1큰술 • 설탕 1/2큰술 • 식초 1/2큰술

두부와 호박에 있는 물기를 꼭 짠 다음 간 쇠고기, 돼지고기, 다진 표고버섯과 양념을 넣어 잘 섞어둔다. 만두피 가장자리에 달걀 흰자를 바른 후 양념해둔 만두소를 한 술 떠서 놓는다. 그 위에 달걀 지단과 잣을 한두 개 넣고 네 모서리를 서로 붙여 모양을 만든다. 만두를 끓는 물에 넣어 삶거나 쪄서 초간장과 같이 낸다.

rice cakes with
vegetables and beef 떡잡채 Tteokjapchae

Tteokjapchae is essentially the same as regular Japchae, which is made from sweet potato noodles, sliced beef, and various vegetables. The uniqueness of Tteokjapchae is that it replaces sweet potato noodles with rice cakes, Tteok, sliced thinly. The chewy pieces of Tteok add a whole different dimension to this dish.

• 1/2 lb rice cakes, cut 2 inches long and cut in half again
• 1/4 lb beef tenderloin, cut into thin strips about 2 inches long
• 2 dried shitake mushrooms, soaked in the warm water to reconstitute for 30 minutes, stems discarded and cut into thin strips
• 1/2 carrot, peeled and cut into thin strips • 1 small onion, cut into very thin strips
• 1/2 bundle enoki mushrooms • 1/2 red bell pepper, cut into very thin strips
• 1/2 green bell pepper, cut into very thin strips
• 1/2 yellow bell pepper, cut into very thin strips

Marinade for beef and mushrooms
• 1 tbsp soy sauce • 1 tsp sugar • 1/2 tsp minced garlic
• 1/2 tsp chopped green onion • 1 tsp sesame oil • 1/8 tsp black pepper

Rice cake seasoning
• 1 tsp soy sauce • 1 tsp sugar • 1 tbsp sesame oil

Mix together ingredients for marinade, pour over the beef and mushrooms, and set aside.

Sauté each vegetable separately in vegetable oil until softened and sprinkle with a little salt to taste. Quickly sauté marinated beef and mushrooms over high heat.

Cook rice cakes in boiling water until soft and rinse in cold water. Mix rice cakes with rice cake seasoning. Combine all the prepared ingredients with rice cakes and mix well.

• 가래떡 300g, 5cm 길이로 잘라 길게 1/4등분한다. • 소고기 안심 150g, 5cm 길이로 가늘게 채 썬다. • 마른 표고버섯 2개, 불린 후 채 썬다. • 당근 1/2개, 가늘게 채 썬다. • 양파 1개(소), 채 썬다. • 팽이버섯 1/2봉지 • 홍피망 1/2개, 채 썬다. • 청피망 1/2개, 채 썬다. • 노란 피망 1/2개, 채 썬다. 고기 버섯 양념 • 간장 1큰술 • 설탕 1작은술 • 다진 마늘 1/2작은술 • 다진 파 1/2작은술 • 참기름 1작은술 • 후추 1/8작은술 떡 양념 • 간장 1작은술 • 설탕 1작은술 • 참기름 1큰술

고기 버섯 양념을 잘 섞은 후 고기와 버섯을 넣어 재어둔다. 각각의 야채를 달궈진 팬에 기름을 두르고 볶아낸 후 소금으로 간을 해둔다. 달궈진 팬에 고기와 버섯을 넣고 센불로 볶아낸다. 끓는 물에 썰어둔 떡을 넣고 부드럽게 될 때까지 삶고 찬물에 헹군 다음 떡 양념을 넣어 버무린다. 볶아놓은 재료와 떡을 섞어 간을 맞춰 접시에 담아낸다.

chive pancakes 부추전 Buchu Jeon

This special dish tastes great, but has a simple, homemade quality due to chives. Many Koreans grow chives in their vegetable gardens since they are easy to cultivate and pick. The cooking time should be less than 20 minutes but the health benefit of chives will last much longer.

• 1 cup chives, chopped • 1 cup shrimp, peeled, de-veined and chopped
• 1/2 cup flour • 1/2 cup water • Pinch of salt • Vegetable oil

Dipping sauce
• 1 tbsp soy sauce • 1/2 tbsp sugar • 1/2 tbsp vinegar

Mix together all the ingredients for the pancakes in a medium sized bowl. Heat vegetable oil in a frying pan over medium heat. Place rounded spoonfuls of the batter into the pan and cook both sides until brown.

• 부추 1컵, 잘게 썬다. • 새우 1컵, 껍질을 벗기고 내장을 뺀 후 잘게 썬다. • 밀가루 1/2컵 • 물 1/2컵 • 소금 조금 • 식용유(지짐용) 초간장 재료 • 간장 1큰술 • 설탕 1/2큰술 • 식초 1/2큰술 초간장 재료를 잘 섞어둔다.

썰어놓은 재료들을 섞어 달궈진 프라이팬에 기름을 넉넉히 두르고 반죽을 한 술씩 동그랗게 놓아 앞뒤로 노릇노릇하게 지져낸다. 밀가루 대신 부침가루를, 새우 대신 다른 해물을 사용해도 좋다.

savory steamed egg custard

계란찜 *Gyeran Jjim*

Gyeran jjim is almost like a savory pudding in appearance and texture. It is extremely light with a wetter, silken feel on the tongue. It's perfect for a first course because of its simplicity and subtle taste. This egg custard is great comfort food and is often fed to babies as well.

- 2 eggs • 2/3 cup water
- 1 tsp salted shrimp juice, salted shrimp can be found in any Korean grocery store
- 1 tsp mirin • 1 tsp sesame oil • Salt • Sugar • Steaming basket • 4 ramekins

Optional for garnish
- Chopped green onion • Chopped red Serrano pepper

Beat together the eggs, water, shrimp juice, mirin, sesame oil, a pinch of salt, and a pinch of sugar. Skim off the foam from the top of the egg mixture. Strain the egg mixture into the ramekins, filling them about 2/3 full.

In a large saucepan, place a steaming basket inside and pour in enough water to just reach the bottom of the steaming basket. The basket should not be submerged and it should not be floating in the water. Place filled ramekins in steaming basket and drape the top of the ramekins with a piece of sturdy plastic wrap to capture the steam. Place the lid on the saucepan and bring water to a boil on medium heat. Steam ramekins for about 7~8 minutes, adjusting according to the size of the ramekin. While it steams you can prepare the garnish. If you do not have green onion or Serrano pepper, you may use whatever you have on hand to garnish the egg jjim. When the egg jjim is completely cooked, sprinkle with the garnish and serve hot.

• 달걀 2개 • 물 2/3컵 • 새우젓 국물 1작은술 • 맛술 1작은술 • 참기름 1작은술 • 소금 약간 • 설탕 약간 선택재료 • 다진 파 • 다진 홍고추

그릇에 달걀, 물, 새우젓 국물, 맛술, 참기름, 소금, 설탕을 넣고 잘 섞어서 체에 걸러 작은 그릇에 2/3 정도씩 부어놓는다. 큰 냄비에 찜기를 넣고 물을 부은 다음 그 위에 달걀 그릇을 놓고 뚜껑을 덮어 중불로 7~8분 정도 찐다(이때 그릇의 크기에 따라 시간을 조절한다). 다진 파와 홍고추로 장식하여 낸다.

pan-fried tofu with beef 두부구이 Dubu Gui

This particular preparation of tofu is an excellent way to bring out the subtle taste of the bean curd itself. Most tofu recipes add marinades or spices that tend to mask the taste of the tofu. Pan fried with oil, the tofu is more than just an accompaniment to the marinated meat inside.

- 1 lb firm tofu, cut into slices about 2 or 3 inches long and 1/2 inch thick
- 1/3 lb beef tenderloin, cut into thin strips about 2 inches long
- 2 green onions, sliced diagonally • 2 cloves garlic, thinly sliced
- 1 tsp salt • Vegetable oil for cooking

Marinade for beef
- 1 tbsp soy sauce • 1 tbsp. brown sugar • 1 tsp sesame oil • 1/2 tsp minced garlic
- 1/2 tsp chopped green onion • Black pepper

Mix together ingredients for marinade, pour over the beef, and set aside. Heat 1 tablespoon of oil in a frying pan and cook beef over high heat until evenly browned, about 3 minutes. Remove from pan.

Sprinkle the salt over the sliced tofu. Cook tofu in a frying pan with vegetable oil on medium heat until golden brown, about 3 minutes on each side. Remove from pan and set aside. Add 1 tablespoon of oil to the pan and cook sliced garlic until light brown. Remove and add sliced green onion and cook for 3 seconds. Transfer slices of tofu to a plate, place cooked beef on top of each slice, and add another slice of tofu on top of the beef, creating a tofu sandwich. Garnish with fried garlic and green onions, serve warm.

• 단단한 두부 1모, 1cm 두께로 얇게 썰어둔다. • 쇠고기 등심 150g, 길게 채 썬다. • 파 2뿌리, 어슷썰기한다. • 마늘 2쪽, 얇게 저민다. • 소금 1작은술 • 식용유(지짐용) 고기 양념장 • 간장 1큰술 • 설탕 1큰술 • 참기름 1작은술 • 다진 마늘 1/2작은술 • 다진 파 1/2작은술 • 후추 약간 • 고기 양념장을 잘 섞어 고기를 재어둔다.

달궈진 팬에 기름을 1큰술 두르고 재어둔 고기를 넣어 약 3분간 볶아놓는다. 썰어둔 두부에 소금을 뿌려둔다. 달궈진 팬에 기름을 두르고 앞뒤로 노릇노릇해질 때까지 약 3분간 지져낸다. 팬을 닦은 후 새로 기름을 두르고 저며 놓은 마늘과 어슷썰기한 파를 넣어 살짝 볶아낸다. 접시에 두부를 놓고 볶아낸 고기를 얹고 두부를 한 켜 더 얹어 두부 샌드위치를 만든 다음 그 위를 볶은 마늘과 파로 장식하여 낸다.

sweet potato noodles
with beef and vegetables 잡채 Japchae

This recipe is by far the most requested recipe in my mother's repertoire. It is an extremely popular party food amongst Koreans and I don't remember a party without it when growing up. The chewy texture of sweet potato noodles makes for an interesting contrast to the rest of the ingredients. Even though the dish requires elaborate preparation, it always makes for a healthy meal.

- 1/4 lb beef tenderloin, cut into thin strips about 2 inches long
- 2 dried shitake mushrooms, soaked in the warm water to reconstitute
  for 30 minutes, stems removed and cut into very thin strips
- 1/2 carrot, peeled and grated • 1 small onion, cut into very thin strips
- 1 large leaf of red cabbage, cut into very thin strips

- 1/2 red bell pepper, cut into very thin strips
- 1 pickling cucumber, seeded and cut into very thin strips • 2 oz sweet potato noodles

Marinade for beef and mushrooms
- 1 tbsp soy sauce • 1 tsp sugar • 1/2 tsp minced garlic • 1/2 tsp chopped green onion
- 1 tsp sesame oil • 1/8 tsp black pepper

Dressing
- 1 tbsp soy sauce • 1 tsp sugar • 1 tbsp sesame oil

Mix together ingredients for marinade, pour over the beef and mushrooms and set aside.

Sauté vegetables separately in vegetable oil. When softened, sprinkle with a little salt to taste. Quickly sauté marinated beef and mushrooms over high heat.

Cook noodles in boiling water until soft and rinse in cold water. Cut into pieces about 4 inches long, and mix with dressing. Combine 1/2 of all the prepared ingredients with noodles and mix well.

Place on a serving plate and garnish with the other 1/2 of the prepared ingredients.

• 쇠고기 등심 120g, 가늘게 5cm 길이로 채 썬다. • 마른 표고버섯 2개, 불려서 가늘게 채 썬다. • 당근 1/2개, 껍질을 벗기고 채 썬다. • 양파 1개(작은 것), 가늘게 채 썬다. • 적양배추 1잎, 가늘게 채 썬다. • 홍피망 1/2개, 가늘게 채 썬다. • 피클오이 1개, 속을 빼고 가늘게 채 썬다. • 당면 2온스 **고기 버섯 양념** • 간장 1큰술 • 설탕 1작은술 • 다진 마늘 1/2작은술 • 다진 파 1/2작은술 • 참기름 1작은술 • 후추 1/8작은술 **무침 양념** • 간장 1큰술 • 설탕 1작은술 • 참기름 1큰술

무침 양념을 잘 섞어 고기와 버섯을 각각 재어둔다. 뜨겁게 달궈진 팬에 기름을 두르고 썰어놓은 야채를 각각 볶아 소금, 후추로 간을 해둔 다음 뜨거운 팬에 고기를 볶아 꺼내고 남은 국물에 버섯을 볶아낸다. 당면을 뜨거운 물에 삶아 부드러워지면 찬물에 헹궈 물기를 빼고 10cm 길이로 자른 후 무침 양념과 볶아둔 재료의 반을 넣어 잘 섞어둔다. 큰 접시 가운데 볶은 재료들과 섞은 잡채를 담고 둘레에 남겨놓은 재료들을 각각 예쁘게 장식하여 낸다. ✿ 죽순이나 양파, 표고버섯을 같은 크기로 썰어서 기름에 살짝 볶아 함께 넣어도 좋다.

Soups & Salads

seaweed soup 미역국 Miyeok Guk

Traditionally this soup is eaten at birthdays or served to women after childbirth to assist in recovery. Like all other sea vegetables, wakame is high in dietary fiber, calcium, and iodine. This soup can be modified to incorporate any seafood such as mussels, baby clams, and anchovies.

• 2 oz dried seaweed, soaked in cold water for 20 minutes • 1 tsp sesame oil
• 1 tsp Korean light soy sauce or salt to taste

Beef stock
• 1/3 lb beef tenderloin • 1 clove garlic, sliced • 1 green onion, white part only
• Salt and pepper to taste • 6 cups water

Soak the beef for the stock in cold water for 30 minutes. Place beef, garlic and green onion for beef stock in a large pot, add the 6 cups of water, and bring to a boil. Reduce heat and simmer for 1 hour, then remove the meat from the broth. Skim off the fat that floats to the top of the broth. Salt and pepper the broth to taste.

Slice the boiled beef into thin strips and marinate with salt, garlic, and sesame oil. Drain seaweed and cut into 2 inch lengths. Heat sesame oil in a thick bottomed saucepan, add seaweed, and stir-fry over high heat for 2 minutes. Pour in prepared beef stock and bring to a boil. Reduce heat to low and simmer for 20 minutes.

Ladle into individual bowls, add marinated boiled beef on top, and serve with cooked rice.

• 마른 미역 30g, 찬물에 20분간 불린다. • 참기름 1작은술 • 국간장 1작은술 또는 소금 육수 • 쇠고기 등심 150g • 마늘 1쪽, 얇게 저민다. • 파 흰 부분 1도막 • 소금 조금 • 후추 조금 • 물 6컵

쇠고기를 30분간 담가 핏물을 뺀 후 큰 냄비에 넣고 마늘, 파, 물 6컵을 넣어 끓인다. 거품을 걷어내면서 1시간 정도 끓인 후 고기는 건져내고 국물은 소금과 후추로 간한다. 고기를 얇게 썰어 다진 마늘과 소금, 참기름으로 간하여둔다. 물에 불려둔 미역을 건져내어 먹기 좋은 크기로 자른다. 달궈진 두꺼운 냄비에 참기름을 두르고 미역을 넣어 약 2분간 볶은 후 준비해둔 육수를 넣고 약 20분간 더 끓인다. 국이 다 끓으면 그릇에 담고 양념해둔 고기를 얹어낸다. ❖ 고기 대신 홍합을 넣어 미역국을 끓여도 맛이 좋다.

rice cake soup 떡국 Tteok Guk

Tteok Guk is a traditional soup made of rice cake slices(long sausage-like rice cake sliced into ovals). It is the essential New Year's Day dish for Korean people. It may not be served with fan-fare, but sitting down with my immediate family with large comforting bowls of Tteok Guk is the best way to welcome the New Year. For Koreans, eating a bowl of Tteok Guk signifies growing one year older. You can also add dumplings to this to make rice cake dumpling soup.

• 8 oz rice cake • 1 egg, separated

Beef stock
• 1/2 lb beef tenderloin • 1 clove garlic, thinly sliced • 1 green onion, white part only
• Salt and pepper to taste • 6 cups water

Seasoning for cooked beef
• 1 green onion, thinly sliced • 1 tsp minced garlic
• 1+1/2 tsp salt • 2 tsp sesame oil • 1/4 tsp black pepper

Soak 1 paper towel in a small amount of oil and lightly oil a small frying pan. Cook egg white and yolk separately, tilting pan to create a thin pancake. Remove from pan and slice thinly to make egg jidan (thinly fried egg used for garnish).

Soak the beef for the stock in cold water for 30 minutes. Place beef in a large pot, add the 6 cups of water, and bring to a boil. Reduce heat and simmer for 1 hour, then remove the meat from the broth. Skim off the fat that floats to the top of the broth. Salt and pepper the broth to taste. Slice the boiled beef into thin strips and marinate with seasonings and set aside.

Pour seasoned stock into another pot and bring to a boil. Add rice cakes and cook for 3 minutes. Ladle into individual bowls, add marinated boiled beef on top, and garnish with egg jidan and sliced green onions.

If you prefer, you can also use chicken stock for the base of this soup.

• 떡 250g • 달걀 1개, 황백을 나누어 풀어둔다. 육수 • 쇠고기 등심 150g • 다진 마늘 1작은술 • 파 흰 부분 1도막 • 소금 조금 • 후추 조금 • 물 6컵 고기 양념 • 파 1뿌리, 어슷썰기한다. • 다진 마늘 1작은술 • 소금 1+1/2작은술 • 참기름 2작은술 • 후추 1/4작은술

달궈진 팬에 기름을 묻힌 종이타월로 프라이팬을 닦아낸 후, 풀어놓은 달걀을 황백으로 나누어 지단을 부쳐 얇게 썰어둔다. 쇠고기를 30분간 찬물에 담가 핏물을 뺀 후 냄비에 넣고 마늘, 파, 물 6컵을 넣어 끓인다. 거품을 걷어내면서 1시간 정도 끓인 후 고기는 건져내고 국물은 소금과 후추로 간한다. 건져낸 고기는 얇게 썰어 파, 다진 마늘, 소금, 참기름으로 간하여 둔다. 냄비에 간을 맞춰둔 국물을 넣고 끓여 떡을 넣은 다음 약 3분간 끓인다. 떡이 다 익으면 그릇에 담고 양념한 고기와 달걀 지단, 어슷 썬 파로 장식하여 낸다. ❖ 닭뼈와 가슴살로 육수를 만들어 떡국이나 만둣국 국물로 사용해도 맛이 좋다.

spinach baby clam soup

시금치조개국 Sigeumchi Jogae Guk

Known as "spinach soup" to my brother and me growing up, this is the one dish, my mother knows, is sure to bring a smile to my face. I absolutely love this soup. I love the tiny chewy pieces of clam, the sharp, earthy taste of Korean Miso and the soft spinach floating in the reddish brown broth. Mixed with rice and a few side dishes, it makes for a perfect dinner.

• 1 lb spinach, washed and cut into half, lengthwise • 8 oz littleneck clam meat

• 2 tbsp doenjang(Korean soybean paste)

• 1 tsp gochujang(Korean hot pepper paste)

• 1 tsp minced garlic • 1 tbsp chopped green onion

• 5 cups any kind of stock, preferably fish stock

In a large pot, add the stock and stir in the doenjang and gochujang until it dissolves. Bring to a boil and cook for about 2 minutes. Add spinach, clam meat, and garlic. Boil over medium high heat for about 3 more minutes. Add green onions and cook for 1 minute longer.

    Serve hot with cooked rice.

• 시금치 450g, 씻은 후 반으로 자른다. • 대합조개 225g 또는 조개 통조림 1캔 • 된장 2큰술 • 고추장 1작은술 • 다진 마늘 1작은술 • 다진 파 1큰술 • 육수 또는 물 5컵

큰 냄비에 물이나 육수를 넣고 된장과 고추장을 풀어 끓인다. 끓기 시작하면 시금치, 조개, 다진 마늘을 넣고 약 3분간 더 끓인 후 썰어놓은 파를 넣고 1분 더 끓인다. ❖ 1. 생조개를 사용할 경우 먼저 소금물에 담가 해감을 시킨 다음, 물에 조개를 넣고 끓여 체에 걸러 국물을 만들어 사용한다. 2. 조개 통조림을 사용해도 좋다.

spicy beef soup 육개장 Yukgaejang

Although Yukgaejang is fairly easy to make, it is quite hard to make a proper one. Yukgaejang is all about ratio and proportion. You have to add the right amount of spiciness to create heat while making sure the soup is still flavorful. I often encounter Yukgaejang that has the right amount of spiciness but a pitifully watery tasting soup. I have never been able to achieve the proper ratio on my own, and it has caused me much frustration. I'm pleased that my mother chose this recipe for this book so that you can escape similar frustration as hers has always been perfect.

- 1 pound beef flank steak or brisket, halved • 8 cups water
- 1/2 large green onion, white part only • 1/4 onion for broth
- 3 clove garlic, sliced • whole black peppercorns
- 2 large green onions, halved lengthwise and cut into lengths • 2 eggs, beaten

Seasoning
- 2 tbsp red pepper powder • 1 tbsp sesame oil
- 2 tbsp light soy sauce • 2 tsp minced garlic • Black pepper to taste

Soak the beef in cold water for 30 minutes. Place the beef, black pepper, onion, garlic, and green onion in a large pot, add the 8 cups of water and bring to a boil. Reduce heat and simmer for 1 hour or until beef is tender. Remove the beef from the pot and shred the beef finely. Bring the beef broth to a boil over medium high heat, and blanch large green onions slightly in boiling broth. Set aside shredded beef and blanched green onions in a bowl.

Combine the seasoning ingredients in a bowl. Pour seasoning mixture over beef and blanched green onions and leave for 10 minutes and then add to the boiling broth. Just before serving, pour the beaten eggs slowly into the soup, stirring gently at the same time.

Serve hot with cooked hot rice.

• 쇠고기(양지머리) 600g • 물 8컵 • 대파 흰 부분 1도막 • 양파 1/4개 • 마늘 3쪽, 얇게 저민다. • 통후추 5알 • 대파 2대, 길게 잘라둔다.
• 달걀 2개, 풀어둔다. 고기 양념 • 고춧가루 2큰술 • 참기름 1큰술 • 국간장 2큰술 • 다진 마늘 2작은술 • 후추 조금

쇠고기를 찬물에 30분 정도 담가 핏물을 빼 둔다. 냄비에 물을 넣고 끓으면 쇠고기, 파, 양파, 후추, 마늘을 넣고 속까지 푹 익도록 1시간 정도 삶아 건진 뒤 결대로 찢어놓고 육수는 체에 걸러놓는다. 냄비에 걸러놓은 국물을 넣어 끓으면 준비해 둔 파를 넣어 살짝 데쳐낸다. 고기와 데친 파를 고기 양념으로 무쳐서 간이 배게 10분 정도 두었다가 끓는 국물에 넣어 한 소끔 끓이고 풀어놓은 달걀을 넣고 다시 살짝 끓여낸다. ❖육개장에 고사리, 숙주, 토란대 등 다른 야채를 넣어서 끓여도 좋다.

tofu hot pot 두부전골 Dubu Jeongol

My mother came up with this recipe because she loves to use tofu in her cooking. It's extremely healthy and at times, challenging to add flavor to. The whole concept behind hot pot is to allow us to choose what we would like to eat and to participate in the cooking process. She also loves the whimsy of the presentation as the hot pot is still bubbling when served at the table.

• 1 lb medium firm tofu, sliced into 1.5 inch cubes

• 1/4 lb beef tenderloin, sliced into thin strips • 1 carrot, peeled and cut into thin strips

• 1 small onion, peeled and cut into thin strips • 1 zucchini, cut into thin strips

• 1/4 lb mushrooms, cut into thin strips

Marinade for beef and mushrooms
• 1 tbsp soy sauce • 1 tsp sugar • 1/2 tsp minced garlic
• 1/2 tsp minced green onion • 1 tsp sesame oil • 1/8 tsp black pepper

Beef stock
• 1/2 lb beef tenderloin • 1 tsp minced garlic • 1 green onion, white part only
• 1 inch thick slice of daikon radish • Salt and pepper to taste • 6 cups water

Soak the beef for the stock in cold water for 30 minutes. Drain and pat dry with a paper towel. Place beef in a large pot, add the 6 cups of water and bring to a boil. Reduce heat and simmer for 1 hour, then remove the meat from the broth. Skim off the fat that floats to the top of the broth. Slice the boiled beef and daikon radish into thin strips. Salt and pepper the broth to taste.

Mix together ingredients for marinade and pour over the beef and mushrooms separately and set aside. Take the sliced boiled beef and daikon slices and layer them on the bottom of a chongol pot. Arrange the marinated raw beef, marinated mushrooms, carrot, onion, zucchini and, tofu over the boiled beef and daikon layer. Pour the hot beef broth over the ingredients and bring to a boil. Serve with cooked rice.

• 두부 1모, 사방 4cm 크기로 도톰하게 썬다. • 쇠고기 150g, 가늘게 채 썬다. • 당근 1개, 껍질을 벗기고 가늘게 채 썬다. • 양파 1개, 채 썬다. • 호박 1개, 얇게 저며둔다. • 새송이버섯 1/2개, 채 썬다. (표고버섯을 사용해도 좋다.) 고기 버섯 양념 • 간장 1큰술 • 설탕 1작은술 • 다진 파, 다진 마늘 각 1/2작은술 • 참기름 1작은술 • 후추 1/8작은술 육수 • 쇠고기 등심 150g • 무 1도막 • 다진 마늘 1작은술 • 파 흰 부분 1도막 • 소금 조금 • 후추 조금 • 물 6컵

쇠고기를 30분간 찬물에 담가 핏물을 뺀 후 냄비에 넣고 무, 마늘, 파, 물 6컵을 넣어 끓인다. 거품을 걷어내면서 1시간 정도 끓인 후 고기와 무는 건져내고 국물은 소금과 후추로 간한다. 건져낸 고기와 무를 얇게 썰어 다진마늘, 파, 소금, 참기름으로 간하여 무쳐둔다. 썰어놓은 쇠고기와 버섯에 각각 고기 버섯 양념을 넣어 재어둔다. 전골냄비나 뚝배기에 삶아 양념해둔 고기와 무, 양념해둔 버섯을 깔고 가운데 양념한 고기를 얹고 주위에 두부와 썰어놓은 야채를 번갈아가며 예쁘게 담은 후 육수를 부어 끓여낸다.

royal casserole

신선로 Sinseollo

Sinseollo is an elaborate dish consisting of meat balls, mushrooms, vegetables and more, cooked in a rich broth. It was served only to the royal family on special occasions and was inaccessible to common people in the "olden days" of Korean history. As a result, it isn't very common and is very complicated to make. My mother wanted to introduce less common types of Korean food to second generation Korean Americans, as well as other people of different ethnicities, so she modified the traditional Sinseollo to be simpler and more accessible.

- 1/4 lb ground beef tenderloin
- 1 zucchini, cut in half and sliced into quarters lengthwise
- 3~4 large shrimps, peeled and deveined • 1 red bell pepper, cut into strips
- 3 shitake mushrooms, soaked in warm water to reconstitute for 30 minutes, stems discarded and cut into halves
- 10 chives or minari(Korean watercress), cut into halves • 1 egg, beaten
- 1/4 lb white fish fillets, slice into pieces 2 in by 3 in size, sprinkle with salt and black pepper
- 2 tbsp flour • 1 egg, beaten

Marinade for beef
- 2 tsp soy sauce • 1/2 tsp sugar • 1/2 tsp minced garlic
- 1 tsp chopped green onion • 1 tsp sesame oil • 1/8 tsp black pepper

Beef stock
- 1/3 lb beef tenderloin • 1 tsp minced garlic • 1 green onion, white part only
- 1 inch thick slice of daikon radish • Salt and pepper to taste • 6 cups water

Marinade for cooked beef and daikon radish
- 1 tsp salt • 1 tsp chopped green onion • 1 tsp minced garlic • 1 tsp sesame oil

Soak the beef for the stock in cold water for 30 minutes and then drain. Place beef, garlic, green onion and daikon radish for stock in a large pot, add the 6 cups of water, and bring to a boil. Reduce heat and simmer for 1 hour, then remove the meat from the broth. Skim off the fat that floats to the top of the broth. Salt and pepper the broth to taste. Combine the ingredients for the Marinade for cooked beef and daikon radish in a bowl and set aside. Slice the boiled beef and daikon radish into thin strips and pour the Marinade over the beef and radish, stirring to combine.

Mix together ingredients for the beef Marinade and pour over the ground beef. Make 1/2 inch diameter meatballs from the marinated ground beef and set aside. Dredge each slice of fish into the flour and then into one beaten egg. Cook in the frying pan and cut into bite size pieces. Dip the chives into the other beaten egg and fry in the well oiled frying pan, cut into bite size pieces. (about 2 inch size)

Take the marinated boiled beef and daikon slices and layer them on the bottom of a shinseol-lo pot. Arrange, in an alternate fashion, the shrimp, mushrooms, white fish, chives, zucchini and red bell pepper over the boiled beef and daikon layer. Garnish with meatballs and pour the hot beef broth over the ingredients and bring to a boil until the meatballs are fully cooked. Serve.

• 쇠고기 등심 다진 것 125g • 호박 1개, 반으로 갈라 길이로 얇게 저민다. • 대하 3~4마리, 껍질을 벗기고 내장을 뺀 후 반으로 가른다. • 홍피망 1개, 씨를 빼고 호박과 같은 크기로 자른다. • 표고버섯 3개, 불려서 반으로 자른다. • 실파 또는 미나리 10줄기 • 달걀 1개, 풀어둔다 • 흰살생선 150g, 얇게 썰어 소금, 후추로 밑간한다. • 밀가루 2큰술 • 달걀 1개, 풀어둔다 고기 양념 • 간장 2작은술 • 설탕 1/2작은술 • 다진 마늘 1/2작은술 • 다진파 1작은술 • 참기름 1작은술 • 후추 1/8작은술 육수 • 쇠고기 등심 150g • 무 1도막 • 다진 마늘 1작은술 • 대파 흰 부분 1도막 • 소금 조금 • 후추 조금 • 물 6컵 고기 무 양념 • 소금 1작은술 • 다진 파, 다진 마늘 각각 1작은술씩 • 참기름 1작은술

쇠고기를 30분간 담가 핏물을 뺀 후 큰 냄비에 넣고 무, 마늘, 파, 물 6컵을 넣어 끓인다. 거품을 걷어내면서 1시간 정도 끓인 후 고기와 무는 건져내고 국물을 소금과 후추로 간한다. 건져낸 고기와 무는 얇게 썰어 다진마늘, 파, 소금, 참기름으로 간하여 무쳐둔다. 간 쇠고기에 고기 양념을 넣어 섞은 다음 지름 1.5cm 크기의 완자를 만들어둔다. 소금 후추로 밑간해둔 생선에 밀가루를 묻히고 달걀을 씌워 부쳐 5cm 길이로 썰어놓는다. 실파나 미나리도 풀어놓은 달걀과 함께 부쳐 생선과 같은 크기로 썰어놓는다. 신선로용 냄비나 뚝배기에 양념해둔 고기와 무를 깔고 그 위에 준비한 재료들을 번갈아 돌려넣고, 사이사이에 고기완자로 장식한 후 육수를 부어 끓여낸다.

soft tofu stew 순두부찌개 Sundubu Jjigae

This stew is always served in a stone pot called "ttukbaegi". I love adding an egg to mine while the soup is still bubbling so it scatters into tender threads of eggs, like in Chinese egg drop soup. Sundubu Jjigae means "uncurdled tofu stew" in Korean. This dish is particularly popular in the winter season because the spiciness provides warmth and it is extremely easy to make.

• 10 oz. sundubu (soft tofu) • 2 oz. pork loin, thinly sliced

• 1/2 cup mixed seafood (shrimp, calamari or scallops) • 3 mussels

• 1 cup water • 1 green onion, sliced diagonally • 1 tsp sesame oil

❖ Sundubu can be found in Korean grocery stores.

Sundubu sauce

• 1 tbsp water • 2 tsp fish sauce

• 1 tbsp coarse hot pepper powder • 1 tsp minced garlic

Combine ingredients for sundubu sauce and set aside.

Heat the sesame oil in a small pot and stir fry the sauce mixture for a few seconds. Add pork and cook for 2-3 minutes, mixing the pork with the sauce. Add water and bring to a boil over high heat. Once it starts to boil, add and continue to boil for about 5 minutes. Spoon in tofu and boil for another 5 minutes. Garnish with sliced green onions and serve immediately.

• 순두부 1봉 • 돼지고기 50g • 해물 1/2컵 (새우, 오징어, 패주) • 홍합 3개 • 물 1컵 • 파 1뿌리, 어슷썰기한다. • 참기름 1작은술 순두부소스 재료 • 고춧가루 1큰술 • 물 1큰술 • 다진 마늘 1작은술 • 멸치액젓 2작은술 순두부소스 재료를 섞어둔다.

달궈진 뚝배기에 참기름을 두르고 섞어둔 소스를 넣어 잠깐 동안 볶은 후 썰어놓은 돼지고기를 넣어 2~3분간 더 볶는다. 고기가 익으면 물을 붓고 센불로 끓이다가 국물이 끓기 시작하면 해물을 넣어 5분 정도 더 끓이면서 순두부를 숟가락으로 떠 넣고 파를 넣은 후 약 5분간 더 끓여낸다. ❖ 1. 순두부에 수분이 많으므로 국물을 너무 많이 넣지 않는다. 2. 굴이나 조개 등 다른 해물을 넣어도 맛있다.

rapini salad 레피니겉절이 Rapini Geotjeoli

The term "salad" is used loosely for this recipe. The rapini with red pepper dressing tastes more like fresh kimchi. My mother developed this recipe because she wanted to find a good alternative vegetable to use when napa cabbage or daikon radish, more commonly used in kimchi, are unavailable. Rapini is not a vegetable widely grown in Korea but is easily found in the states. It tastes sweet, but tart, and is very refreshing.

• 1 bunch Rapini • 1 tbsp salt

Dressing

• 1+1/2 tbsp hot pepper powder • 2 tbsp Basic sauce (vinegar 5: sugar 4: salt 1)

• 1/2 tbsp fish sauce • 1 tsp toasted sesame seeds

• 1 green onion cut into 1inch pieces, then shredded • 1 tsp minced garlic

Wash Rapini under running water and drain. Put Rapini in a bowl and sprinkle the salt evenly over it. Let sit for 30 minutes and then rinse and drain well. Mix together all of the ingredients for the dressing and pour over Rapini, mixing well.

• 레피니 1단(또는 겉절이용 야채 1단) • 소금 1큰술 무침 양념 • 고춧가루 1+1/2큰술 • 베이직소스 2큰술 (식초 5: 설탕 4: 소금 1) • 멸치 액젓 1/2큰술 • 볶은 깨 1작은술 • 파 1뿌리, 길게 채 썬다. • 다진 마늘 1작은술

레피니를 흐르는 물에 깨끗이 씻어 소금을 고루 뿌려둔다. 30분 후, 물에 헹궈 물기를 빼둔다. 무침 양념을 골고루 섞어 물기를 뺀 레피니에 넣어 잘 버무려낸다.

tofu salad
with soy dressing

두부샐러드 Dubu Salad

This salad is surprisingly light and refreshing with a simple combination of tofu and vegetables. It's great for a quick, healthy lunch and the soy dressing is absolutely delicious. I use any extra dressing as a sauce for fresh vegetables and chilled noodles. It keeps well in the refrigerator, so you can make the sauce and freeze it to save time.

- 1 lb medium firm tofu • 1 cup egg plant, chopped
- 1/2 cup red onion, chopped
- 1/2 cup red bell pepper, chopped • Olive oil for cooking
- Korean watercress or any kind of green for garnish (optional)

Soy dressing
- 2 tbsp soy sauce • 1 green onion, chopped
- 1 clove garlic, minced • 1 tsp toasted sesame seeds
- 1 tbsp sugar • 1 tbsp vinegar • 1 tsp sesame oil

Mix together all ingredients for Soy dressing and set aside.

Prepare the warm tofu by placing the tofu in a metal strainer with a long handle and lowering it into a pot of boiling water. Cook for about 20~30 seconds or until heated through, then remove and drain. Cut tofu into 1+1/2 inch size cubes. Heat a frying pan and add a spoonful of olive oil. Sauté chopped vegetables until softened. Arrange tofu pieces on a serving plate with vegetables on top and pour the soy dressing over them to taste. Garnish with Korean watercress.

• 두부 1모 • 다진 가지 1컵 • 다진 붉은 양파 1/2컵 • 다진 홍피망 1/2컵 • 올리브유 조금 • 파슬리 또는 미나리순 (장식용) 간장소스 • 간장 2큰술 • 다진 파 1큰술 • 다진 마늘 1작은술 • 볶은 깨 1작은술 • 설탕 1큰술 • 식초 1큰술 • 참기름 1작은술 간장소스를 잘 섞어둔다.

두부를 뜨거운 물에 20~30초 동안 담가 살짝 데쳐낸다. 두부를 가로세로 3cm, 높이 3cm 크기로 썰어둔다. 달궈진 프라이팬에 올리브유를 두른 다음, 잘게 썰어 둔 야채를 넣어 볶아낸다. 접시에 두부를 놓고 그 위에 볶아낸 야채를 얹은 후 간장소스를 끼얹고, 파슬리 또는 미나리로 예쁘게 장식하여 낸다.

fresh tofu salad 생두부야채무침 Saengdubu Yachae Muchim

This dish is best served cold. The combination of fresh vegetables, tofu, and soy dressing is very delicious. This dish is low in calories and full of flavor. Plus it is very easy to make.

- 8 oz tofu • 1 cup lettuce, cut into thin strips
- 1/2 cucumber, cut into thin strips • 1/2 carrot, cut into thin strips
- 1/2 package of radish sprouts • 1/4 red bell pepper, cut into thin strips

Soy dressing
- 2 tbsp soy sauce • 1 green onion, chopped • 1 clove garlic, minced
- 1 tsp toasted sesame seeds • 1 tbsp sugar • 1 tbsp vinegar • 1 tsp sesame oil

Mix together all ingredients for Soy dressing and set aside.

Prepare the warm tofu by placing the tofu in a metal strainer with a long handle and lowering it into a pot of boiling water. Cook for about 20~30 seconds or until heated through, then remove and drain. Cut tofu into triangle shaped pieces, about 1+1/2 inches in size. Mix cut vegetables together and set aside. Arrange tofu pieces on a serving plate with vegetables and pour the soy dressing over them to taste.

• 두부 1/2모 • 상추 1컵, 채 썬다. • 오이 1/2개, 채 썬다. • 당근 1/2개, 채 썬다. • 무순 한 줌 • 홍피망 1/4개 , 채 썬다. 간장소스 • 간장 2 큰술 • 다진 파 1큰술 • 다진 마늘 1작은술 • 볶은 깨 1작은술 • 설탕 1큰술 • 식초 1큰술 • 참기름 1작은술 간장소스 재료를 잘 섞어둔다.

끓는 물에 두부를 넣어 20~30분 동안 데쳐낸 다음 1.5cm 크기의 삼각형 모양으로 썰어둔다. 접시 가장자리에 두부를 두른 후 채 썰어둔 야채를 섞어 가운데 담고 간장소스와 함께 낸다. 먹기 직전에 소스를 뿌린다. ❖ 쑥갓, 브로콜리, 어린 상추 등 다른 채소를 사용해도 좋다.

grilled vegetables with soy dressing 야채구이 Yachae Gui

This recipe was the first one my mother conceptualized with me when we first began this book. She loved the beautiful Italian grilled vegetables we were served at a cousin's wedding reception and wanted to adapt them for this book, but with Korean flavors and ingredients.

• 1 Korean zucchini • 1 regular eggplant or 2 Japanese eggplants
• 1/2 red bell pepper • 1/2 yellow bell pepper • 10 Korean mild peppers
• 1/4 lb mushrooms • 1 tbsp olive oil

Soy dressing

• 2 tbsp soy sauce • 1 green onion, chopped • 1 clove garlic, minced
• 1 tsp toasted sesame seeds • 1 tbsp sugar • 1 tbsp vinegar
• 1 tsp sesame oil

Mix together all ingredients for Soy dressing and set aside.

Slice zucchini, eggplant, red bell pepper, yellow bell pepper, and mushrooms into 1/4 inch thick slices. On a hot grill, cook each slice, about 3 minutes on each side. Lightly brush olive oil on each side. Arrange vegetables on a serving plate and pour the soy dressing over them to taste.

• 호박 1개 • 가지 2개 • 홍피망 1/2개 • 노랑 피망 1/2개 • 꽈리고추 10개 • 새송이버섯 1/2개 • 올리브유 1큰술 간장소스 • 간장 2큰술 • 다진 파 1큰술 • 다진 마늘 1작은술 • 볶은 깨 1작은술 • 설탕 1큰술 • 식초 1큰술 • 참기름 1작은술 간장소스 재료를 잘 섞어둔다.

호박, 가지, 홍피망, 노랑 피망, 새송이버섯을 0.5cm 두께로 길게 썰어둔다. 뜨겁게 달궈진 그릴이나 팬 위에 준비해 둔 야채를 올려 앞뒤로 3분씩 구운 후 올리브오일을 바르고 접시에 예쁘게 담아 그 위에 간장소스를 적당히 올려낸다.

seasoned soybean sprouts

콩나물무침 Kongnamul Muchim

Kongnamul is my mother's favorite side dish. She serves it as a side dish with every meal without fail. When you make it, you can add hot pepper, which is common in Korea. However, this recipe does not include it because my mother likes to enjoy the taste of bean sprout itself and the hot pepper tends to drown out the subtler flavors.

• 1 lb soybean sprouts, roots trimmed • 1/2 cup water
• 1 green onion, sliced diagonally • 1/2 tsp minced garlic
• 1 tsp toasted sesame seeds • 1 tbsp sesame oil • 1+1/2 tsp salt

Wash the soybean sprouts a few times, removing any bean husks. Place in a pot, add water and salt, cover tightly. Bring to a boil for about 3~5 minutes. Do not lift the cover during boiling because the soybean sprouts will develop an unpleasant taste. Drain.

In a large bowl, combine remaining ingredients except the sesame oil. Add the soybean sprouts and toss well. Then add sesame oil and mix again to coat.

Serve warm or chilled.

• 콩나물 450g, 꼬리를 다듬는다. • 물 1/2컵 • 파 1개, 어슷썰기한다. • 다진 마늘 1/2작은술 • 볶은 깨 1작은술 • 참기름 1큰술 • 소금 1+1/2작은술

다듬은 콩나물을 씻어 냄비에 담고 물 반 컵과 소금을 넣어 뚜껑을 덮은 후 3~5분간 삶는다. (삶는 동안 뚜껑을 열면 비린내가 나므로 열지 않는다.) 물기를 빼고 참기름을 뺀 나머지 양념을 넣어 무친 다음 마무리로 참기름을 넣어 다시 한번 잘 무친다.

Meat

braised beef in ginger soy sauce

쇠고기장조림 Soegogi Jangjorim

Soegogi Jangjorim, like Myolchi Bokem, is a home-style side dish that is usually served as comfort food, rather than to guests. In my college years, my best friend would often shred the braised beef into pieces, heat it up in the microwave with some rice and a little of the gingery soy braising liquid, and we would eat it as a sort of quick Bibimbap(a bowl of rice topped with various assortments of meat and vegetables). Even now the smell of Jangjorim reminds me of college days and make-shift meals in the dorm.

• 1 lb skirt steak or flank steak • 6 cups water • 3, 1 inch pieces of ginger, thinly sliced
• 1/2 cup soy sauce • 2 tbsp sugar

Cut the beef into 2 inch square pieces. Place the beef in a pot with the water and ginger, and boil for 10 minutes. Periodically skim off the residue as it rises to the top. Cover and simmer until the meat is just tender about 1+1/2 hours. Remove the beef and strain the stock. Set aside.

Shred the meat and return it to the pot. Add 1+1/2 cups of stock, boiled ginger, soy sauce, sugar and bring to a boil. Reduce the heat and simmer over low heat for 20 minutes, until the beef is very tender. Serve with cooked rice as a side dish.

• 쇠고기(치맛살, 양지) 450g • 물 6컵 • 생강 3도막, 얇게 저민다. • 간장 1/2컵 • 설탕 2큰술

고기를 5cm 크기로 잘라둔다. 냄비에 썰어둔 고기, 물과 생강을 넣어 10분간 끓인다. 끓는 동안 떠오르는 거품을 떠낸 다음 뚜껑을 덮어 약불로 1시간 30분 정도 더 끓인 후 고기를 건져내어 약간 식힌 후 결대로 찢어놓고 국물을 받쳐 놓아 둔다. 다른 냄비에 찢어둔 고기와 끓인 생강을 건져 같이 넣고 받쳐둔 육수 1+1/2컵, 간장, 설탕을 넣어 약불로 20분간 더 졸인다.

pan-fried meat and tofu cakes

고기완자전 Gogi Wanja Jeon

These cakes with ground meat and chopped vegetables are similar to small hamburger patties. It is a favorite of children and non-Koreans as it is delicious and has a familiar taste. My mom regards this dish as a welcoming side dish for families and friends.

- 1/2 lb ground pork • 1/4 lb ground beef
- 1 package of hard tofu, mashed into small pieces with a fork and water squeezed out
- 4 green onions, green parts only, chopped • 1/3 carrot peeled, chopped
- 1/2 onion, chopped • 2 tbsp flour • 2 eggs, beaten with a pinch of salt

Marinating sauce

• 1 tsp salt • 1 tsp sugar • 1 tsp ginger juice
• 1/4 tsp black pepper • 1/2 tbsp toasted sesame seeds
• 1/2 tbsp sesame oil • 1 tbsp mirin or cheongju

In a large bowl, combine beef, pork, tofu, green onion, carrot, and onion with marinating sauce. Mix well and then shape mixture into a cylinder, wrap tightly, and freeze. After about 1 hour, unwrap the cylinder, and cut into 1/4 inch thick slices. Put flour in a separate bowl and dredge each piece until all surfaces are lightly covered.

Heat a large frying pan over medium heat. Add about 2 or 3 teaspoons of oil to the pan and place each flour-covered slice into the beaten egg. When completely covered, put into the hot pan and cook until both sides are golden brown. It should take about 1~2 minutes per side.

Place cooked patties on a paper towel to drain. Periodically refresh the pan with new oil and repeat the process for the rest of the slices.

• 간 쇠고기 225g • 간 돼지고기 225g • 두부 1모, 물기를 짜고 잘게 부순다. • 실파 4뿌리, 파란 부분만 잘게 다진다. • 당근 1/3개, 껍질을 벗긴 후 잘게 다진다. • 양파(작은 것) 1/2개, 잘게 다진다. • 밀가루 2큰술 • 달걀 2개, 소금을 넣고 잘 풀어둔다. 양념 • 소금 1작은술 • 설탕 1작은술 • 생강즙 1작은술 • 후추 1/4작은술 • 볶은 깨 1/2큰술 • 참기름 1/2큰술 • 맛술 1큰술

큰 그릇에 준비해 둔 모든 재료와 양념을 넣어 잘 섞어 동그란 원통 모양을 만든 다음 랩으로 말아 1시간 정도 얼린다. 얼려놓은 반죽을 꺼내어 1cm 두께로 썰어 녹여둔다. 앞뒤로 밀가루를 묻힌 후 풀어놓은 달걀에 적셔, 달궈진 프라이팬에 기름을 두르고 속이 잘 익을 때까지 노릇하게 지져낸다(앞뒤로 약 1~2분간씩 지지면 된다). ❖ 1. 지져낸 완자전을 종이타월 위에 얹어 기름을 뺀다. 2. 중간 중간 팬을 종이타월로 닦아내고 새로 기름을 둘러야 깨끗하게 지져진다.

73

braised chicken with vegetables

닭찜 Dakjjim

Dakjjim refers to a seasoned and simmered chicken, much like a French coq au vin. You can use any vegetable you wish in place of the potatoes and carrots. The simmering allows the chicken to absorb the seasoning, resulting in a tender and more flavorful taste. The skin and bones of the chicken are left on to help create the delicious sauce.

• 1.5 lb Cornish hen • 1 potato, cut into 1 inch pieces with edges rounded

• 1 carrot, cut into 1 inch pieces with edges rounded

• 3 dried shitake mushrooms, soaked in warm water to reconstitute and quartered

Marinating sauce

• 2 tbsp soy sauce • 1 tbsp sugar • 1 tbsp chopped green onion

• 1 tsp minced garlic • 1 tsp ginger juice • 1 tsp toasted sesame seeds

• 1 tbsp sesame oil • 1/2 tsp ground black pepper

• 1 tbsp mirin • 1/3 cup water

Mix together all ingredients for Marinating sauce in a bowl and set aside.

Rinse Cornish hen well in cold water. Dry with paper towel and chop into 2 inch pieces. Blanch potatoes and carrots in boiling water and drain.

Cook chicken in a frying pan on high heat until golden brown. Pour the Marinating sauce over the chicken, mixing to coat thoroughly. Cook for an additional 10 minutes. Add water, potatoes, carrots, and mushrooms to the pan and bring to a boil. Then lower the heat and simmer until tender, about 10 more minutes. Remove from heat and serve hot.

• 어린 닭 1마리 • 감자 1개, 3cm 크기로 동그랗게 깎는다. • 당근 1개, 3cm 크기로 동그랗게 깎는다. • 마른 표고버섯 3개, 불려서 4등분 해놓는다. 조림장 간장 2큰술 • 설탕 1큰술 • 다진 파 1큰술 • 다진 마늘 1작은술 • 생강즙 1작은술 • 볶은 깨 1작은술 • 참기름 1큰술 • 후추 1/2작은술 • 맛술 1큰술 • 물 1/3컵 조림장 재료를 잘 섞어둔다.

닭을 깨끗이 씻어 종이타월로 물기를 닦은 후, 5cm 크기로 잘라둔다. 깎아놓은 감자와 당근은 끓는 물에 데쳐놓는다. 달궈진 팬에 기름을 두르고 잘라놓은 닭을 놓아 앞뒤로 노릇하게 지진 다음 섞어놓은 조림장을 부어 10분 정도 끓이고 불을 줄인다. 데쳐놓은 감자, 당근, 버섯과 물을 넣어 약 10분간 더 졸여낸다.

barbecued pork ribs

돼지갈비구이 Dwaeji Galbi Gui

The use of honey water is the most important part of the marinating process in this recipe. Make sure that the meat is evenly covered and thoroughly marinated. If you add the sesame oil first, it will overpower the taste of the meat and not allow the marinade to soak into the meat. If you combine the ingredients all at once, the sugar will not caramelize properly and will compromise the texture of the meat. These ribs tastes best when grilled, but you can also cook it in a frying pan.

• 2+1/2 lbs pork ribs • 4 tbsp honey • 4 tbsp water

Marinating sauce

• 1 tbsp mirin • 2 tbsp Korean hot pepper paste (gochujang) • 1+1/2 tbsp soy sauce

• 1 tbsp chopped green onion • 2 tsp minced garlic • 1/4 tsp black pepper

• 1 tbsp toasted sesame seeds • 3 tbsp sesame oil

Combine Korean hot pepper paste, soy sauce, mirin, sesame seeds, black pepper, green onion, and minced garlic to make marinade in a separate bowl and set aside.

Stir together honey and water until honey is mostly dissolved. Pour honey water mixture over the meat and mix until meat is well coated. Let sit for about 5 minutes. Pour prepared marinade over the meat and mix until it is well coated. Then add sesame oil and mix again to coat.

Let meat marinate 30 minutes, or if you wish, you can marinate it overnight. Cook meat on a grill, or if you prefer you may cook it in a frying pan, but grilling is best.

• 돼지갈비 1200g • 꿀 4큰술 • 물 4큰술 갈비 양념장 • 맛술 1큰술 • 고추장 2큰술 • 간장 1+1/2큰술 • 다진 파 1큰술 • 다진 마늘 2작은술 • 후추 1/4작은술 • 볶은 깨 1큰술 • 참기름 3큰술 그릇에 참기름을 뺀 양념장 재료를 잘 섞어둔다.

꿀과 물을 섞어 꿀이 다 녹으면 갈비에 부어 밑간하여 재워둔다. 밑간해둔 갈비에 양념장 재료를 넣어 잘 섞고 참기름을 넣어 다시 한번 잘 무친다. 30분간 두었다가 달군 그릴이나 팬에 놓아 갈비가 잘 익을 때까지 굽는다. ❖ 하루 전에 재워 냉장보관 했다가 구우면 간이 잘 배어 더 좋다.

royal barbecued pork 맥적 Maekjeok

Maekjeok was considered a special food for the royal family. Maekjeok predates bulgogi, the more familiar form of grilled Korean barbecue. The distinctiveness of this recipe lies in the use of Korean Miso (Korean soybean paste). It marks pleasant change from routine soy sauce.

• 1 lb pork loin • 2 tbsp honey • 1 tbsp mirin • 2 tbsp water
• 1 tbsp doenjang (Korean soybean paste) • 1 tbsp light soy sauce or soy sauce
• 1 tbsp chopped green onion • 1 tsp minced garlic
• 1 tbsp toasted sesame seeds • 1 tbsp sesame oil

Cut the pork into slices about 1/8 inch thick. Marinate with honey, water, and mirin. Combine the doenjang, soy sauce, chopped green onion, minced garlic and sesame seeds to make the seasoning sauce. Mix the pork with the seasoning sauce and then add the sesame oil and mix again. Cook seasoned pork on a hot grill, turning often.

• 돼지등심 450g • 꿀 2큰술 • 맛술 1큰술 • 물 2큰술 • 된장 1큰술 • 국간장 1큰술 또는 간장 1큰술 • 다진 파 1큰술 • 다진 마늘 1작은술 • 볶은 깨 1큰술 • 참기름 1큰술

돼지고기를 불고깃감으로 얇게 썰어둔다. 꿀, 맛술, 물을 섞어 고기에 넣어 밑간하고 된장, 간장, 파, 마늘, 깨를 섞어 고기에 넣어 무친 다음 참기름을 넣어 다시 한번 잘 섞어둔다. 달궈진 팬이나 그릴에 양념에 재둔 고기를 앞뒤로 완전히 익을 때까지 굽는다.

grilled beef with chive salad

로스구이 | Roseu Gui

Roseu Gui is a recipe that I turn to when I am having a lot of people over for dinner. It's very easy to make because the beef is simply grilled or roasted without seasoning or stuffing. Remember to cut the beef as thinly as possible for a better taste. If you don't ask the butcher to cut it for you, you can always freeze it and cut it thinly with a knife.

- 2/3 lb beef rib eye (shabu shabu cut)
- 2 cups garlic chives or chives, cut into 2 inch pieces

Dressing
- 1 tbsp soy sauce • 1 tbsp vinegar • 1 tbsp sugar
- 1 tsp hot pepper powder • 1 tsp toasted sesame seeds
- 1 tbsp sesame oil

Put the chives in a bowl and set aside. Cook beef on hot grill or pan fry until well done. Mix chives with dressing shortly before eating and serve with cooked beef.

• 소고기 안심 300g (샤브샤브용) • 부추 2컵, 5cm 길이로 자른다. 부추 양념장 • 간장 1큰술 • 식초 1큰술 • 설탕 1큰술 • 고춧가루 1작은술 • 볶은 깨 1작은술 • 참기름 1큰술 양념장재료를 잘 섞어둔다.

5cm 길이로 자른 부추를 접시에 담아둔다. 달궈진 팬이나 그릴에 고기를 구워 고기가 익으면 먹기 직전 접시에 담긴 부추에 섞어둔 양념장을 부어 고기와 함께 내어 고기에 부추를 싸먹는다. 부추 대신 파를 썰어 찬물에 담가 매운맛을 뺀 다음 소스에 무쳐 곁들여도 좋다.

Korean kebabs 산적구이 Sanjeok Gui

Sanjeok is a Korean Kebab made of seasoned meat, mushrooms and vegetables. You can vary the type of vegetables used. It is similar to Fish Sanjeok but more common because it is easier to prepare.

- 1/3 lb beef (round steak or flank steak) • 3 green onions • 1/2 carrot
- 3 shitake mushroom, soaked in warm water to reconstitute and drained
- 1/2 red bell pepper • Pine nuts or toasted sesame seeds for garnish(optional)

Marinade
- 2 tbsp soy sauce • 2 tsp sugar • 1 tsp minced green onion
- 1/2 tsp minced garlic • 1 tsp sesame oil • 1/8 tsp black pepper

Additional Equipment

• Bamboo skewers

Soak skewers in cold water for about an hour. Cut beef into slices about 1/4 inch thick and then cut slices into strips about 3 inches long and 3/4 inch wide. Cut the root end off of the green onions and cut them into 3 inch pieces. Repeat with the carrot, mushrooms and red pepper. Blanch carrot slightly in boiling water.

Combine all marinade ingredients in a bowl. Pour marinade over beef and vegetables and leave for 10 minutes. Place ingredients on skewers by impaling one end of each 3 inch piece. You can order the ingredients any way you wish, keeping in mind that you will want to have 2 or 3 pieces of meat, and about 9 pieces total on each skewer. Cook each skewer in a large frying pan or grill.

Garnish with chopped pine nut or toasted sesame seeds.

• 쇠고기 150g • 파 3뿌리 • 당근 1/2개 • 말린 표고버섯 3개, 불려놓는다. • 홍피망 1/2개 • 꼬치 • 잣 또는 볶은 깨 (장식용) 양념장 • 간장 2큰술 • 설탕 2작은술 • 다진 파 1작은술 • 다진 마늘 1/2작은술 • 참기름 1작은술 • 후추 1/8작은술

꼬치를 찬물에 1시간 정도 담가둔다. 고기를 넓이 2cm, 길이 7cm, 두께 0.5cm로 썰어놓는다. 파, 당근, 양파, 홍피망을 고기와 같은 크기로 썰어놓는다. 뜨거운 물에 당근을 살짝 데쳐놓는다. 양념장 재료를 잘 섞어 썰어둔 재료들을 넣고 10분 간 재어둔다. 색을 맞춰 꼬치에 차례대로 끼워 달궈진 팬이나 그릴에 지져 다진 잣이나 깨로 장식하여 낸다. ❖ 1. 꼬치 1개 에 고기를 2~3개 정도 끼우면 더 좋다. 2. 재료들을 꼬치에 끼워 밀가루를 묻히고 달걀을 씌워 전으로 지져도 좋다.

broiled beef patty 섭산적 Seopsanjeok

Seopsanjeok is very similar to hamburger patties. When my mother was in elementary school and went on school picnics, 90% of her classmates would bring Gimbap (Korean rice rolls), while my grandmother would pack my mother little sandwiches or a lunch box with Seopsanjeok. She absolutely hated it because Gimbap was her favorite food and she didn't understand why her mother packed such fancy lunches. Later in life she has come to appreciate her elementary school lunches, and that is why she decided to include this Seopsanjeok recipe.

- 1/2 lb ground beef • 1/4 lb tofu • 1 tbsp chopped green onion
- 1 tsp minced garlic • 2 tsp sugar • 1 tbsp soy sauce • 1/4 tsp salt
- 2 tsp mirin • 1/8 tsp black pepper • 1 tbsp sesame oil
- 2 tsp toasted sesame seeds
- 1 tbsp chopped pine nut • 1 cup shredded lettuce

Squeeze the water from the tofu. Transfer tofu to a bowl, mash with a fork, and mix with ground beef. Add all the rest of the ingredients and combine until mixture becomes sticky. Form beef mixture into 4 patties. Heat a large frying pan with the sesame oil and cook patties to desired doneness, about 5 minutes on each side. Remove from the pan, serve with shredded lettuce, and garnish with chopped pine nut.

• 쇠고기 다진 것 250g • 두부 125g • 다진 실파 1큰술 • 다진 마늘 1작은술 • 설탕 2작은술 • 간장 1큰술 • 소금 1/4작은술 • 맛술 2작은술 • 후추 1/8작은술 • 참기름 1큰술 • 볶은 깨 2작은술 • 다진 잣 1큰술 • 채 썬 상추 1컵

두부의 물기를 뺀 후, 으깨어 고기와 같이 섞는다. 나머지 재료를 모두 넣어 잘 섞은 다음 치대어놓는다. 4등분 하여 칼등으로 두드려 평평하고 둥글넓적하게 만든 다음 달궈진 팬에 참기름을 두르고 앞뒤로 약 5분간 구워 낸다. 팬에서 꺼내어 채 썬 상추와 다진 잣을 장식하여 접시에 담아낸다.

Korean-style barbecued beef

불고기 구이 Bulgogi Gui

When most people think of Korean food, they think of kimchi and Bulgogi. Bulgogi is the most common form of Korean barbecue. Famous for its sweet marinade, there are many variations of this dish. It is usually accompanied by fresh vegetables such as lettuce.

- 2 lb beef tenderloin or sirloin • 3 tbsp brown sugar • 4 tbsp cold water
- 1 tbsp chopped green onion • 4 tbsp soy sauce
- 1 tbsp mirin • 2 tsp toasted sesame seeds • 1 tbsp sesame oil
- 1/4 tsp ground black pepper • 1 tsp minced garlic
- 1 tsp ginger juice, ginger juice can be created by grating gingerroot finely over a bowl and collecting the resulting juices

Slice the tenderloin super-thin.

Combine green onion, soy sauce, mirin, sesame seeds, black pepper, ginger juice, and minced garlic to make marinade in a separate bowl and set aside.

Stir together brown sugar and water until sugar is mostly dissolved. Pour sugar water mixture over the meat and mix until meat is well coated. Let sit for about 5 minutes. Pour marinade over the meat and mix until it is well coated. Then add sesame oil and mix again to coat.

Let meat marinate 30 minutes, or if you wish, you can marinate it overnight. Cook meat on a grill, or if you prefer you may cook it in a frying pan, but grilling is best.

• 쇠고기 불고깃감 900g • 흑설탕 3큰술 • 물 4큰술 • 맛술 1큰술 양념장 • 간장 4큰술 • 다진 마늘 1큰술 • 생강즙 1작은술 • 다진 파 2큰술 • 후추 1/2작은술 • 통깨 1큰술 • 참기름 2큰술

고기의 지방을 제거하고 원하는 두께로 얇게 썬다. 흑설탕 3큰술, 물 4큰술, 맛술 1큰술을 섞은 다음 설탕이 녹을 때까지 저어 밑간 양념을 만들고, 여기에 고기를 골고루 무친다. 분량대로 재료를 섞어 양념장을 만든다. 이때 거름망을 이용해서 건더기를 제거하면 고기를 더 깔끔하게 구울 수 있다. 밑간해둔 고기에 참기름을 뺀 나머지 양념을 섞어준 다음 참기름을 넣어 다시 잘 섞는다. 양념이 고루 배면 뜨겁게 달군 그릴이나 브로일러, 또는 석쇠에 구워낸다.

braised short ribs 갈비찜 Galbijjim

Galbijjim is a Korean steamed dish made with beef. In Michigan, where we grew up, the winters are often very cold. My mother used to make this for us to warm us up after school. It is a very hearty and rich tasting dish similar to a beef stew. We would often make this for holidays such as New Year's Day.

- 1.5 lb beef shortribs
- 1/4 daikon radish, diced in 1 inch pieces with edges rounded
  (they should look somewhat like small, peeled potatoes)
- 1 carrot, also diced in 1 inch pieces with edges rounded
- 10 cooked chestnuts: can be replaced with 1 peeled and diced potato
- 6 dried Asian dates, these can be found in an Asian grocery store
- 3 dried shitake mushrooms (soaked to reconstitute), quartered
- 3 slices of peeled ginger

Optional ingredients

- 10 peeled gingko nuts • 1 tsp pine nuts for garnish

Marinating sauce

- 5 tbsp soy sauce • 3 tbsp lightly packed brown sugar
- 2 tbsp chopped green onion • 1 tbsp minced garlic
- 1 tbsp toasted sesame seeds • 1 tbsp sesame oil
- 1 tsp ground black pepper • 1 tbsp mirin

Mix together all ingredients in a bowl and set aside.

Rinse beef shortribs well in cold water. In a 3+1/2 qt. saucepan, put ginger in 6 cups of cold water and bring to a boil. Add the meat and continue to boil until it is tender, about 45 minutes to an hour. As the ribs tend to be a bit fatty, occasionally skim the oil from the surface of the liquid.

After the meat is tender, remove the ribs from the pot and reserve the cooking broth in a separate container. Put the ribs back into the pot and pour the marinating sauce over the ribs, mixing to coat thoroughly. Add 2 cups of the reserved broth, daikon radish, carrot, dates, and shitake mushrooms to the pot and bring to a boil. Then lower the heat and simmer until vegetables are tender, about 30 minutes.

In the last few minutes of cooking, add chestnuts, gingko nuts and return to a boil. Remove from heat and serve hot.

• 갈비 600g • 무 1도막 • 당근 1개 • 밤 10개 • 은행 10개 • 대추 5개 • 불린 표고버섯 3개 • 잣 1큰술 • 생강 2쪽 갈비 양념장 • 간장 5큰 술 • 흑설탕 3큰술 • 다진 파 2큰술 • 다진 마늘 1큰술 • 통깨 1작은술 • 참기름 1큰술 • 후추 1작은술 • 맛술 1큰술

갈비를 찬물에 담가 핏물을 제거하고 칼집을 넣는다. 끓는 물에 생강을 저며 넣고 갈비를 넣어 삶아 건진 다음 준비한 양념장을 고루 끼얹어 잠시 간이 배도록 둔다. 무와 당근은 밤 크기로 둥글게 돌려깎기를 해서 데쳐놓는다. 냄비에 양념해둔 갈비를 넣고, 갈비 삶았던 물 2컵을 자작하게 부은 다음 깎아놓은 무와 당근, 불려놓은 표고버섯을 넣고 한소끔 끓인다. 은행, 밤, 대추를 넣어 다시 한번 끓여낸다. 잣과 지단으로 장식하여 내면 좋다.

ginseng chicken soup 삼계탕 Samgyetang

This is a traditional chicken soup. Special ingredients, such as ginseng and dates are important for taste and appearance. Traditionally, Koreans eat this on the hottest summer days as it gives them the energy boost they often lose from the over bearing heat of the day. You can take the leftovers and turn it into a rice porridge that our family often eats for breakfast.

• 1 cornish game hen, rinsed and patted dry, taking care to rinse the cavity thoroughly

• 1/3 cup sticky rice, soaked in water for 30 minutes and drained

• 3 cooked chestnuts • 2 cloves of garlic • 2 dried Asian dates • 1 dried ginseng root

• 8 cups chicken bone stock, when making stock for this soup,
  it is best to boil the bones with celery and garlic

• Salt • Pepper • Chopped green onion

In a 3+1/2 to 4 qt. saucepan, add dried ginseng root to stock and bring to a boil. In the meantime, stuff the cavity of the hen with the garlic, dates, chestnuts, and rice. Do not stuff the hen too full as the rice will expand while cooking. Cut a slit in the skin on either side of the body cavity of the hen. Stick the end of each leg through the slit on the opposite side, crossing the legs and closing up the cavity. Then tuck each wing underneath the body, much like preparing a turkey for roasting.

Add the hen to the pot and continue to boil, covered, for 30 minutes, occasionally skimming the oil from the surface. Lower the heat and boil for at least 1 more hour.

If you would like to cook more rice with the soup, you can fill an empty loose leaf tea bag with rice and add it to the soup to cook alongside the hen.

Add salt, pepper, and chopped green onion to taste and serve. This recipe can be doubled or tripled very easily. One hen usually serves about two people.

• 영계 1마리(500g), 미국에서는 Cornish game hen을 쓴다. • 찹쌀 1/3컵 • 밤 3개 • 마늘 2쪽 • 대추 2개 • 인삼 1뿌리 • 닭뼈육수 8컵 • 소금 • 후추 • 다진 파

닭을 핏기가 완전히 빠지도록 뼛속까지 깨끗이 씻은 후 꽁지를 자르고 양옆 배를 잘라 구멍을 하나씩 내어놓는다. 찹쌀을 2시간 정도 불려 인삼, 대추, 밤 등과 같이 닭 뱃속에 넣고 다리를 X자 모양으로 꼬아 뚫어놓은 구멍에 끼워넣어 속이 빠지지 않도록 한다. 날개는 몸통 뒤쪽으로 넣어 고정시킨다. 냄비에 닭뼈육수를 넣고 끓기 시작하면 준비해놓은 닭을 넣어 센 불에 30분 정도 끓이면서 위에 뜨는 기름과 거품을 걷어낸 다음 불을 줄여 1시간 정도 더 푹 끓인다. 찰밥을 더 원할 경우 불린 찹쌀을 티백에 반쯤 채워넣어 함께 더 끓인다. 그릇에 푹 끓인 닭을 담고 국물을 부은 후 송송 썰은 파, 소금, 후추와 함께 낸다. ❖ 1. 삼계탕을 닭뼈육수로 끓이면 오래 끓이지 않아도 국물 맛이 진해지고, 고기의 맛도 좋아진다. 2. 닭뼈육수는 평상시 뼈가 붙은 가슴살이나 다릿살을 사서 발라낸 후 냄비에 물을 붓고 푹 고아 얼려두었다가 필요할 때 녹여 쓴다. 3. 육수를 만들 때 양파나 셀러리를 넣고 끓이면 닭의 잡냄새를 없앨 수 있다.

Seafood

skewered fish 어산적 Eosanjeok

This traditional dish is similar to Korean Kebabs. It is filled with alternating layers of white fish with marinated ground meat. The layers are skewered together and either pan-fried or grilled.

- 1/2 lb white fish • 1 tsp salt • 1 tsp sesame oil • Black pepper
- 1/4 lb ground beef tenderloin

Marinade for beef
- 2 tsp soy sauce • 1/2 tsp sugar • 1/2 tsp minced garlic • 1 tsp minced green onion
- 1 tsp sesame oil • 1/8 tsp black pepper • 1 tsp chopped pine nuts

Chives or parsley for garnish
- Bamboo skewers

Soak skewers in cold water for about an hour. Cut the fish into pieces 1/4 inch thick and 3 inches long and season the fish pieces with the salt, sesame oil, and black pepper. Season the ground beef with beef marinade and set aside. Skewer the fish pieces leaving space between each one to be filled with the meat. Fill each space with the seasoned beef by creating a meatball around the skewer. Lightly pound the skewered food with knife. Cook each skewer in a large frying pan or on a grill.

Garnish with chopped pine nut or chopped chives.

흰살생선 250g • 소금 1작은술 • 참기름 1작은술 • 후추 약간 • 간 쇠고기 125g **고기 양념장** • 간장 2작은술 • 설탕 1/2 작은술 • 다진 마늘 1/2작은술 • 다진 파 1작은술 • 참기름 1작은술 • 후추 1/8작은술 • 다진 잣 1작은술 • 실파 또는 파슬리 (장식용) • 꼬치

꼬치를 찬물에 1시간 정도 담가둔다. 생선을 0.5cm 두께와 7cm 길이로 썰어 소금, 후추, 참기름으로 밑간해 둔다. 다진 고기에 양념장을 부어 무쳐둔다. 꼬치에 생선을 간격을 두어 3개를 꽂은 다음 그 사이사이에 양념 해둔 고기로 채워 고기와 생선이 잘 붙도록 고기와 생선을 칼등으로 두드려준다. 준비된 꼬치를 달군 팬에 구 워낸다. 위에 다진 잣, 실파 또는 파슬리로 장식하여 낸다.

spicy squid with vegetables

오징어볶음 Ojingeo Bokkeum

This hot and spicy dish is stir-fried in Korean chili sauce. For this recipe, you can replace the squid with octopus if squid is hard to obtain, but squid is more commonly used. It's perfect as a topping for steamed rice. Squid is very popular with Korean people, it is often eaten dried, as a sort of squid-jerky.

• 1 large squid tube (body only), cut open and cleaned

• 4 small green chilies or 1/2 green bell pepper, cores and seeds removed, cut into strips

• 1/4 red bell pepper, cut into strips • 1/2 carrot, peeled and cut into strips

• 1/2 onion, thinly sliced • 1 tsp minced garlic

Sauce

• 1 tsp mirin • 1 tbsp soy sauce • 1 tbsp ground red pepper

• 1 tsp gochujang (Korean hot pepper paste) • 2 tsp sugar

• 1 tsp toasted sesame seeds • 1 tbsp sesame oil

Mix together all ingredients for sauce except sesame oil and set aside.

Using the tip of knife, score the side of the squid that curls inward in a crisscross pattern.

Bring a large pot of water to a boil. Add the squid and cook until it just starts to curl. Drain and slice into strips.

Heat the 1 tbsp of sesame oil in a frying pan and add garlic and stir fry for 10 seconds.

Add vegetables and stir fry for 2 minutes, then add squid and cook for 2 more minutes.

Pour prepared sauce over the squid and vegetables and mix until well coated and cook for 1 minute. Then add sesame oil and mix again to coat.

Serve warm with cooked rice.

• 오징어(몸통·대) 1마리 • 풋고추 4개 또는 청피망 1/2개, 씨를 빼고 채 썬다. • 홍피망 1/4개, 채 썬다. • 당근 1/2개, 채 썬다. • 양파 1/2개, 얇게 썬다. • 다진 마늘 1작은술 소스 • 맛술 1작은술 • 간장 1큰술 • 고춧가루 1큰술 • 고추장 1작은술 • 설탕 1작은술 • 볶은 깨 1작은술 • 참기름 1큰술 참기름을 뺀 모든 재료를 잘 섞어둔다.

오징어 몸통을 깨끗이 씻어 껍질을 벗기고 안쪽에 가로세로 칼집을 넣은 후 한입 크기로 잘라 끓는 물에 살짝 데쳐둔다. 달군 팬에 참기름을 두르고 다진 마늘을 넣어 볶아 향기름을 만든다. 썰어놓은 야채를 넣어 약 2분간 볶은 후 오징어를 넣어 다시 2분간 더 볶는다. 오징어와 야채에 소스를 넣고 더 볶은 후 참기름을 넣어 잘 섞어 접시에 담아낸다.

stir- fried anchovies with peppers

멸치볶음 Myeolchi Bokkeum

Myeolchi Bokkeum is a homey and rustic side dish. It is a savory combination of salty and sweet and also has a great crunch. The smaller the anchovies, the better it tastes. It's a great source of calcium so it's a must-have for families with small children.

- 2 cups dried anchovies
- 2 jalapeno peppers or Korean green hot peppers, sliced 1/8 inch thick
- 1 tbsp cooking oil

Sauce ingredients
- 2 tbsp soy sauce • 1 tbsp honey • 1 tsp mirin
- 1 tsp toasted sesame seeds • 1 tsp sesame oil • 1/8 tsp black pepper

Stir fry the anchovies and peppers lightly in an oiled pan and set aside.

In a separate pot, combine all the sauce ingredients and bring to boil until the sauce is bubbling. Pour bubbling sauce into anchovies and peppers and stir fry a little more until all of the ingredients are mixed well.

• 지리멸치 2컵 • 매운 풋고추 2개, 얇게 썰어둔다. • 식용유 1큰술 소스 • 간장 2큰술 • 꿀 1큰술 • 맛술 1작은술 • 볶은 깨 1작은술 • 참기름 1작은술 • 후추 1/8 작은술

달궈진 팬에 기름을 두르고 멸치와 고추를 넣어 볶는다. 다른 냄비에 소스재료를 넣고 중불에 끓여 거품이 나기 시작하면 볶아놓은 멸치와 고추를 넣고 섞어낸다.

baked fish patties

오븐에 구운 생선야채전 Baked Saengseon Yachae Jeon

Saengseon Jeon refers to any fish patties or small pancakes made with fish. Traditionally, it's prepared with white fish. However, my mother puts her own spin on it by adding vegetables and other seafood. Making several small pancakes can be time consuming, so my mother came upon the idea of using muffin tins to prepare the jeon. Baking the jeon does not compromise the quality and it is infinitely more convenient. You can prepare larger quantities at once and you can cook other things while the jeon is in the oven. This makes it easier for people who have little time to prepare an otherwise time consuming dish.

• 1/4 lb cod, chopped • 1/4 lb shrimp, shelled, veins removed, and chopped
• 1/2 carrot, peeled and chopped. • 4 green onions, green parts only, chopped
• 1 tbsp flour • 1 egg • 1/4 tsp salt • 1/8 tsp black pepper
• 1/4 red bell pepper, chopped, for garnish

Preheat oven to 450 F. Lightly grease a muffin pan with vegetable oil.

Thoroughly mix together all the ingredients except red pepper. Spoon about 1 tablespoon of the mixture into the prepared muffin cups and garnish with chopped red pepper on top. Bake about 7 minutes and serve warm.

In the alternative, you can make these jeon by cooking them in a frying pan. Just spoon about 1 tablespoon of the mixture into a hot pan and cook for about 2 minutes on each side.

  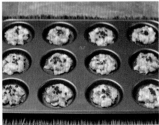

• 대구 150g, 잘게 썰어둔다. • 새우 150g, 껍질을 깐 후 내장을 빼고 다진다. • 당근 1/2개, 껍질을 벗긴 후 잘게 다진다. • 실파 4뿌리, 푸른 부분만 잘게 썬다. • 밀가루 1큰술 • 달걀 1개 • 소금 1/4작은술 • 후추 1/8작은술 • 홍피망 1/4개 또는 붉은고추 1개, 씨를 빼고 잘게 썬다. (장식용) • 무순 조금 (장식용)

오븐을 섭씨 200도로 예열하고 머핀팬에 기름을 발라둔다. 홍피망을 뺀 모든 재료를 잘 섞어 기름을 발라둔 머핀팬에 1큰술씩 놓고 위에 다진 홍피망을 조금 얹어 예열해둔 오븐에 넣어 7분간 구워낸다. 오븐이 없을 경우 달군 프라이팬에 기름을 넉넉히 두르고 1큰술씩 동그랗게 놓아 앞뒤로 약 2분간씩 또는 노릇노릇해질 때까지 지져낸다. ❖ 1. 대구 대신 동태나 광어 등 다른 흰살생선을 사용해도 좋다. 2. 머핀팬이 없을 경우 쿠키팬을 사용해도 좋다.

pan-fried scallop 패주전 Paeju Jeon

Pan-fried scallops are the most delicious version of Korean seafood patties or pancakes. They are made with sliced scallops, sprinkled with flour, and dipped in egg before pan-frying.

Optional Ingredients

Rinse scallops in cold water and pat dry with paper towel. Then slice scallops lengthwise into 1/4 inch slices, each scallop should make about four "discs". Put flour in a separate bowl and dredge each disk until all surfaces are lightly covered, making sure to keep each disk intact.

Heat a large skillet over medium heat. While the pan heats, beat the egg with a pinch of salt. Add about 2 or 3 teaspoons of oil to the pan and place each flour-covered scallop disk into the beaten egg. When completely covered, put into the hot pan and cook until both sides are golden brown. It should take about 1~2 minutes per side.

Place cooked scallop jeon on a paper towel to drain. Periodically refresh the pan with new oil and repeat the process for the rest of the scallops.

Optional

If you would like to add a little spice to your scallop jeon, you can garnish each jeon with thinly sliced red Serrano pepper, sliced green onion, or some Italian parsley leaves. After you place the egg dredged scallop into the pan, place the some of the pepper, green onion, or parsley on the side of the scallop facing up. When you flip the scallop to cook the other side, the egg should help the additional ingredients adhere to the scallop, making a tasty and attractive garnish.

Note

In the interest of time, you may cut and dredge the scallops in flour the night before and store them covered in the refrigerator overnight. As the scallop jeon is best eaten right after they are made, you can dip the scallops in egg and fry them shortly before serving. Serve these with a dipping sauce made of 1 tbsp soy sauce, 1/2 tbsp sugar, and 1/2 tbsp rice vinegar.

• 패주 큰 것 350g • 달걀 1개 • 밀가루 3큰술 • 소금 조금 • 식용유 또는 올리브유 (부침용) • 잘게 썬 홍고추, 실파, 파슬리 (장식용)

패주를 찬물에 씻어 종이타월로 물기를 빼준다. 물기를 뺀 패주를 동그랗게 0.5cm 두께로 얇게 저민다. 밀가루를 묻히고 달걀을 씌워 달궈진 팬에 기름을 두르고 부친다. 종이타월에 놓고 기름을 뺀 후 접시에 담아 홍고추, 파, 파슬리 등으로 장식하여 낸다. ❖ 하루 전에 미리 밀가루에 묻혀 냉장보관했다가 먹기 직전 달걀에 씌워 지져내면 간편하다.

seafood and green onion pancake 해물파전 Haemul Pajeon

Haemul Pajeon is very versatile because you use almost any kind of seafood. My mother prefers to use glutinous rice flour in this recipe because it gives the pancake a better texture and flavor. It also creates an undertone of sweetness that complements the taste of seafood nicely. This dish is very popular as a snack especially on rainy days.

- 5 shrimps, peeled and deveined • 1/2 of one small squid, thinly sliced
- 5 mussels, shredded • 3 scallops, shredded • 8 green onions, cut into 5 inch pieces
- 3 eggs • 1/3 cup sweet rice flour or rice flour • 1/3 cup flour
- Vegetable oil • 1 red pepper, seeded and chopped (garnish)
- 1 green onion, cut diagonally into 1 inch pieces (garnish)

Dipping sauce
- 1 tbsp soy sauce • 1/2 tbsp sugar • 1/2 tbsp vinegar

Mix all the ingredients for the dipping sauce in a bowl and set aside.

Put eggs and both flours in a large bowl and mix well. Add squid, mussels, shrimp, and scallops, and mix. Heat a large frying pan over medium heat and add about 2 tablespoons of vegetable oil. When the oil is hot, bundle half of the green onions, dip them into the batter and spread them on the pan and let it cook about 1 minute. Then pour the half of batter on top, garnish with chopped red hot pepper and cover, cooking for about 3 minutes. Remove the cover, add 1 tablespoon of vegetable oil to the pan around the edge of the pancake and flip it. Continue to cook for another 3~4 minutes or until golden brown on both sides. Repeat with the rest of the batter and green onions. Serve hot with dipping sauce.

• 새우 5개, 껍질을 벗기고 내장을 빼둔다. • 오징어 작은 것 1/2마리 • 홍합 5개, 잘게 썬다. • 패주 3개, 잘게 썬다. • 파 8뿌리, 10cm 길이로 자른다. • 달걀 3개 • 찹쌀가루 또는 쌀가루 1/3컵 • 밀가루 1/3컵 • 식용유(부침용) 장식용 재료 홍고추 1개, 씨를 빼고 다진다. • 파 1뿌리, 어슷썰기한다. 초간장 • 간장 1큰술 • 설탕 1/2큰술 • 식초 1/2큰술 초간장 재료를 섞어둔다.

큰 그릇에 달걀을 풀어 찹쌀가루와 밀가루를 섞고, 썰어둔 해물을 넣어 잘 섞어둔다. 달궈진 팬에 기름을 2큰술 두르고 준비해놓은 파의 반을 넣어 1분 정도 익힌 다음 그 위에 반죽을 붓고 썰어놓은 홍고추와 파로 장식한 후 뚜껑을 덮고 3분 정도 더 익힌다. 뚜껑을 열어 팬 주위에 기름을 1큰술 두르고 뒤집어 3~4분 정도 또는 노릇노 룻해질 때까지 더 지진다. 파전이 다 익으면 초간장과 같이 낸다.

stuffed clams 조개찜 Jogae Jjim

Stuffed clams are a favorite traditional Korean dish. My mother loves this preparation of clams because of its delicate taste. These are perfect for an appetizer or first course.

- 5 large clams • 1/8 lb beef sirloin, chopped
- 1/2 package medium firm tofu • 1 tbsp chopped red bell pepper
- 1 tbsp chopped chili pepper • 1/4 tsp salt • 1 tsp toasted sesame seeds
- 1 tsp chopped green onion • 1/2 tsp minced garlic
- 1 tsp sesame oil • 1/8 tsp black pepper • 1 beaten egg

Vinegar soy sauce

- 1 tsp soy sauce • 1/2 tsp sugar • 1/2 tsp vinegar

Soak the clams in salt water overnight in the refrigerator, so that they spit out the sand they often retain. Clean the clams and scald them in boiling water. Remove the clam meat from the shell and chop it finely. Clean the shells, brush with oil and lightly flour them, setting aside.

Squeeze out the excess water from the tofu (bean curd) and mash with a fork. Mix all the ingredients well. Fill the trimmed shells with the mixture and garnish with parsley. Pour a little of the beaten egg over each stuffed shell. You should use about one tablespoon total. Place the stuffed shells on a steamer rack in the steamer and steam for 10 minutes. Serve hot with vinegar soy sauce.

• 큰 조개 5개 • 다진 쇠고기 50g • 두부 1/2모 • 다진 홍피망 1큰술 • 다진 고추 1큰술 • 소금 1/4작은술 • 볶은 깨 1작은술 • 다진 파 1작은술 • 다진 마늘 1/2작은술 • 참기름 1작은술 • 후추 1/8작은술 • 달걀 1개, 풀어놓는다. 초간장 • 간장 1작은술 • 설탕 1/2작은술 • 식초 1/2작은술

조개를 소금물에 담가 냉장고에 하룻밤 놓아두어 해감시킨 다음 끓는 물에 넣어 살짝 데쳐낸다. 조갯살을 떼어내어 잘게 다지고 껍질은 깨끗하게 씻어 물기를 닦은 다음 기름을 발라 밀가루를 뿌려놓는다. 두부에 있는 물기를 제거한 후 잘게 다지고 달걀을 뺀 나머지 재료들을 다져놓은 조개와 같이 잘 섞어 준비해둔 껍데기 위에 한 숟가락 담고 그 위에 달걀물을 얹어 찜기에 놓고 10분간 쪄낸다. 기호에 따라 초간장을 곁들여낸다. ❖ 원래는 대합조개로 만들던 것인데 다른 조개나 패주로 만들어도 좋다.

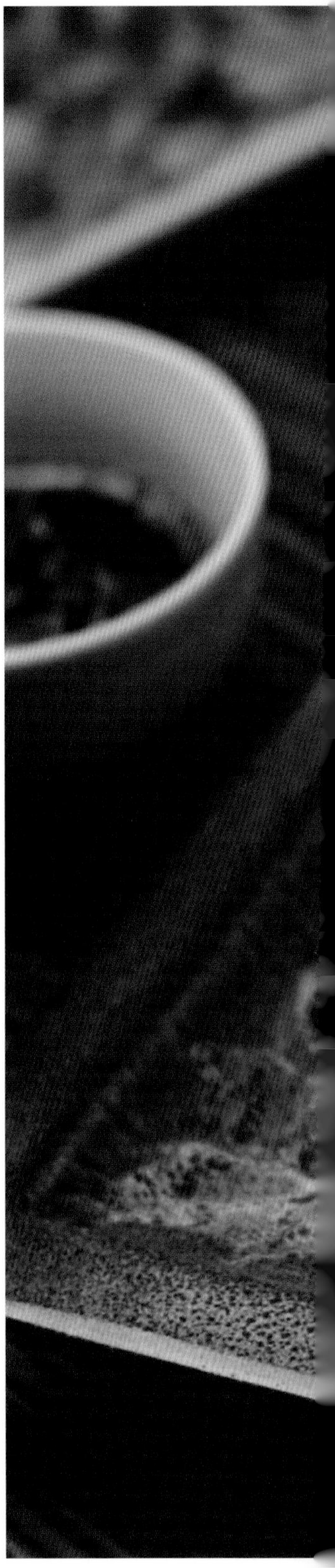

broiled red chili shrimp
and scallops

대하패주양념구이 | Daeha Paeju Yangnyeom Gui

Shrimp and scallops are my mother's favorite seafood, and this recipe is a great way to cook them. She loves spicy food, and the red chili marinade provides a kick that is a nice contrast with the sweetness of the seafood without overpowering it. When cooking the shrimp, remember that simply adding the marinade to the pan will not sufficiently spread the flavor: you must brush each shrimp individually.

- 8 fresh large shrimp, washed and drained • 1 lb sea scallops
- All purpose flour, to dust the scallops • 1 tbsp soy sauce • 1 tbsp sesame oil
- Vegetable oil for cooking
- Scallop shells, Parsley, Lemon and Lime for garnish (optional)

Red chili marinade

- 2 tbsp sugar • 2 tbsp mirin • 2 tbsp gochujang (Korean hot pepper paste)
- 2 tbsp soy sauce • 2 tsp chopped green onion • 1 tsp minced garlic
- 2 tbsp water • 2 tsp toasted sesame seeds

Combine Korean hot pepper paste, sugar, soy sauce, mirin, 20 sesame seeds, green onion, and garlic in a separate bowl to make the marinade and set aside.

In another small bowl combine 1 tablespoon of soy sauce and 1 tablespoon of sesame oil and set aside.

De-vein the shrimp by splitting the back of each shrimp and removing the innards. Season the scallops with salt and pepper and then lightly dust with flour. Heat the oil in a large frying pan, briefly cook both sides of the shrimp until half cooked. Brush each shrimp with the soy sauce and sesame oil mixture and cook for an additional minute. In a cleaned frying pan, briefly cook both sides of the scallops until half cooked. Add the shrimp back to the pan and brush half of the marinade onto the shrimp, pouring the rest of the marinade into the pan, and continue to cook while mixing, until the shrimp and scallops are coated well. Place shrimp on a plate, and place each scallop on a scallop shell. Garnish with parsley, lemon and lime slices and serve.

• 큰 새우 8개, 씻어 물기를 뺀다. • 패주 450g • 밀가루 2큰술 • 간장 1큰술 • 참기름 1큰술 • 식용유 (지짐용) • 패주껍질, 파슬리, 레몬, 라임 (장식용 : 선택) **구이양념** • 설탕 2큰술 • 맛술 2큰술 • 고추장 2큰술 • 간장 2큰술 • 다진 파 2작은술 • 다진 마늘 1작은술 • 물 2큰술 • 볶은 깨 1작은술 구이양념 재료를 잘 섞어둔다. 다른 그릇에 간장 1큰술과 참기름 1큰술을 섞어둔다.

새우등을 갈라 내장을 빼고 껍데기가 붙은 채로 펼쳐놓는다. 패주에 소금과 후추로 간을 한 후 밀가루를 묻혀놓고, 달궈진 팬에 반을 가른 새우를 놓아 앞뒤로 살짝 익힌 후 섞어놓은 간장, 참기름소스를 발라 1분간 더 익혀준다. 달궈진 다른 팬에 식용유를 두르고 패주를 놓아 앞뒤로 반쯤 익혀준 다음, 준비해둔 새우를 같이 넣고 그 위에 구이양념을 발라 다 익을 때까지 더 지진다. 접시에 새우를 놓고 파슬리로 장식하여 낸다. 패주를 패주껍질 위에 놓고 저며놓은 레몬과 라임으로 장식하여 내거나 패주껍데기가 없을 경우 접시에 예쁘게 담아낸다.

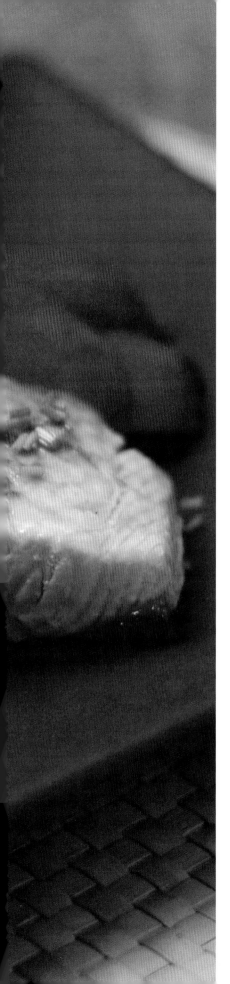

grilled salmon

연어구이 Yeoneo Gui

When I come to visit, my mom tries to make my favorite dishes. This is my favorite; a simple yet tasty way to prepare salmon. This grilled salmon is dressed with salt and sesame oil, which helps bring out the taste of the salmon.

• 1 pound salmon • 1 tsp sea salt • 1 tbsp mirin or rice wine
• 2 tbsp sesame oil or vegetable oil • 1/2 lemon
• Grilled vegetables (optional)

Clean the salmon and dry with paper towel. Cut into 2 inch wide pieces and sprinkle with mirin and sea salt. Let sit for an hour or until the salt has been mostly absorbed. Coat the salted fish with sesame oil or spray with vegetable oil and broil the fish on a heated grill. Garnish with lemon slices and grilled vegetables, serve hot.

• 연어 450g • 바다소금 1작은술 • 맛술 1큰술 • 참기름 2큰술 또는 식용유 • 레몬 1/2개 • 구운 야채 (선택)

연어를 깨끗이 씻어 종이타월로 물기를 닦고 5cm 넓이로 잘라 소금과 맛술을 뿌려둔다. 1시간 정도 두었다가 다 질어지면 참기름을 바르거나 식용유를 발라 뜨겁게 달궈진 그릴이나 팬에 구워낸다. 구운 야채와 함께 레몬으로 장식하여 낸다. ❖ 연어에 레몬주스와 소금을 뿌려 재어 두었다가 기름을 발라 구워도 맛있다.

Rice & Noodles

dried seaweed rolls 김밥 Gimbap

Gimbap looks like Japanese maki but is different in several ways. The rice is marinated with sesame oil rather than vinegar and cooked beef is used instead of raw fish. It's a very common lunch for school and family picnics. Like sandwiches, it's easy to carry and eat.

- 1/2 lb beef, sliced sirloin is best
- 2 eggs, beaten with a generous pinch of salt, cooked into a sheet,
  and sliced into thin strips
- 1 carrot, peeled and cut into thin strips • 1 lb spinach, blanched with water squeezed out
- 2 cups sushi rice, cooked and mixed with 1 tbsp sesame oil and 1/2 tbsp salt
- Nori seaweed sheets • Vegetable oil • Salt

Seasoning for beef

- 1 tbsp brown sugar • 1 tbsp water • 1 tsp minced garlic
- 1 tbsp soy sauce • Ground black pepper
- 1/2 tsp toasted sesame seeds • 1 tbsp sesame oil

Make Filling

Sauté carrots in a hot skillet in vegetable oil and a generous pinch of salt. In a separate bowl, mix spinach with 1/2 teaspoon of salt and 1 tablespoon of sesame oil. Trim the fat from the beef and mix together with brown sugar and water, coating well. Add garlic, a pinch of ground pepper, 1/2 teaspoon of sesame seeds, soy sauce and mix thoroughly. Pour over meat and add 1 tablespoon of sesame oil and coat each piece. Cook meat in a hot skillet until browned, cool slightly, and cut into long strips. Set carrots, spinach, beef and egg aside.

Assembling Gimbap

Place nori sheet on a bamboo rolling mat. Spread about 1/2 cup of rice in a thin, even layer on the seaweed, starting at the base of the sheet closest to you, and working your way up, leaving about 1+1/2 inch of seaweed uncovered at the top. Place a small portion of each ingredient in a horizontal line across the middle of the rice layer. Lift up the base end of the seaweed and mat and roll forward, lifting the end of the mat to prevent it from sticking to the rice, similar to making a jelly roll. Use the mat to push the seaweed around the fillings, creating a cylinder. When you reach the uncovered 1+1/2 inch of nori at the top, dampen the edge with a touch of water to help the roll seal together. Slice into 1/2 inch circles and serve.

• 쇠고기 250g • 달걀 2개, 소금을 넣고 풀어 지단으로 두껍게 부쳐 길게 썰어둔다. • 당근 1개, 껍질을 벗긴 후 길게 썰어둔다. • 시금치 1단, 데쳐서 물기를 빼둔다. • 밥 4공기, 뜨거울 때 참기름 1큰술과 소금 1/2작은술을 넣어 섞어둔다. • 김밥용 김 고기 양념 • 흑설탕 1큰술 • 물 1큰술 • 간장 1큰술 • 다진 마늘 1/2작은술 • 후추 조금 • 소금 조금 • 볶은 깨 1/2작은술 • 참기름 1큰술

달궈진 팬에 썰어둔 당근을 볶은 후 소금으로 간한다. 데쳐놓은 시금치에 소금 1/2작은술과 참기름 1큰술을 넣어 무쳐둔다. 쇠고기를 고기 양념으로 무쳐 달궈진 팬에 볶아낸 후 길게 채 썰어둔다. 김발 위에 김을 놓고 반 컵 정도의 밥을 김의 2/3정도만 얇게 편 후 가운데 준비해둔 재료를 놓고 돌돌 만다.

ver. 2 Japanese style
dried seaweed rolls

일식 김밥 Japanese Style Gimbap

- 5 dried shitake mushrooms, soaked in the 1 cup warm water to reconstitute for 30 minutes, water reserved, stems discarded
- 2 eggs, beaten with a generous pinch of salt, cooked into a sheet, and sliced into thin strips
- 1 carrot, peeled and cut into thin strips • 1 cucumber, cut into thin strips
- 2 cups sushi rice, cooked and mixed with 2 tbsp Basic sauce (vinegar 5 : sugar 4 : salt 1)
- Nori seaweed sheets • Vegetable oil • Salt

Seasoning for mushroom, carrot
- 2 tbsp soy sauce • 2 tbsp sugar
- 1 tbsp mirin • 1 cup mushroom water

Make Filling

Place soy sauce, sugar, mirin, and the water you used to reconstitute the mushrooms into a small pot and bring it to a boil over medium heat. Add mushrooms and boil them in the mixture for about 10 minutes. After 10 minutes add the carrots to the pan and cook both carrots and mushrooms for another 5 minutes. Take the carrots and mushrooms out of the pan and set aside to cool. When the carrots and mushrooms are cool, squeeze the remaining liquid from them and slice the mushrooms into thin strips.

Assembling Gimbap

Place nori sheet on a bamboo rolling mat. Spread about 1/2 cup of rice in a thin, even layer on the seaweed, starting at the base of the sheet closest to you, and working your way up, leaving about 1+1/2 inch of seaweed uncovered at the top. Place a small portion of each ingredient in a horizontal line across the middle of the rice layer. Lift up the base end of the seaweed and mat and roll forward, lifting the end of the mat to prevent it from sticking to the rice, similar to making a jelly roll. Use the mat to push the seaweed around the fillings, creating a cylinder. When you reach the uncovered 1+1/2 inch of nori at the top, dampen the edge with a touch of water to help the roll seal together. Slice into 1/2 inch circles and serve.

• 말린 표고 5개, 불려둔다. • 당근 1개, 껍질을 벗기고 가늘고 길게 썰어둔다. • 오이 1개, 가늘고 길게 썰어둔다. • 달걀 2개, 풀어서 계란말이를 해둔다. • 소금 조금 • 식용유 • 뜨거운 밥 2공기 • 단촛물 2큰술 (식초 5 : 설탕 4 : 소금 1) • 표고, 당근 조림장 (간장 2큰술, 설탕 2큰술, 청주 1큰술, 표고버섯 불린 물 1컵)

뜨거운 밥에 단촛물을 넣고 주걱으로 고루 섞으면서 부채질을 하여 식혀둔다. 달걀을 잘 풀어 소금을 넣고 기름 두른 팬에 붓고 계란말이를 해서 길게 썰어둔다. 조림장에 불린 표고를 넣고 조려 어느 정도 조려지면 길게 썬 당근을 넣어 살짝 익을 정도로 조려낸다. 김발 위에 김을 놓고 반 컵 정도의 밥을 김의 2/3 정도만 얇게 편 후 가운데 준비해둔 재료를 놓고 돌돌 만다.

rice topped with fish eggs 알밥 Albap

Albap is a version of bibimbap that is served with raw fish eggs and vegetables in a hot pot. The heat from the pot cooks the ingredients together and the rice on the bottom and the sides of the bowl becomes brown, crispy, and delicious, much like the best part of a good paella. Albap is the Korean version of a Japanese hot pot and is extremely versatile, as many other things can be substituted for most of the ingredients.

• 4 cups cooked short grain rice

• 2 tbsp sesame oil • 1 tsp salt

• 2 cups napa cabbage kimchi

• 1 tsp sesame oil • 1/2 tsp sugar

• 1/2 tsp toasted sesame seeds

• 1/2 pound flying fish eggs

• 1/2 pound salted pollack eggs

• 1 cup green onions (green parts only), chopped

• 1 cup Korean watercress stems, chopped

• 4 egg yolks • 1 tsp sesame oil

Season the cooked rice in a bowl with the sesame oil and salt, mix well and set aside.

Chop the cabbage kimchi, squeeze out the liquid, and mix with sesame oil, sugar, and toasted sesame seeds. Peel the skin off of the salted pollack eggs and break the eggs apart.

To serve

Put marinated rice into 4 hot pots and arrange the other ingredients over the rice, placing the egg yolk over the top after all the other ingredients have been arranged. Heat the pot until the rice begins to sizzle. Serve hot and mix well to eat.

• 밥 4공기 • 참기름 2큰술 • 소금 1작은술 • 잘게 썬 김치 2컵 • 참기름 1작은술 • 설탕 1작은술 • 볶은 깨 1/2작은술 • 날치알 125g • 명란젓 125g • 다진 실파잎 1컵 • 다진 미나리 1컵 • 달걀노른자 4개 • 참기름 1작은술

밥에 참기름과 소금을 넣고 비벼놓는다. 잘게 썰어놓은 김치의 물기를 짜고 참기름, 설탕, 볶은 깨를 넣어 잘 무쳐둔다. 명란의 껍질을 벗기고 알만 빼둔다. 달궈놓은 뚝배기에 참기름을 두른 후 밥을 넣고 그 위에 준비해둔 재료를 예쁘게 담고 달걀노른자를 가운데 놓은 뒤 불에 올려 지직 소리가 나면 불을 끈다.

steamed rice with beef and vegetables 생야채고기비빔밥 Saengyachae Gogi Bibimbap

This is a simple way to make ordinary steamed rice extraordinary. It is extremely fresh with tender shreds of vegetables, delicious marinated beef and rice. It is infinitely less work than other traditional bibimbaps because the vegetables are not individually marinated. My mother's method of plating here is great if you want a simple yet elegant dish for guests, but you can also pile the ingredients haphazardly in bowls for a quick meal for yourself.

- 1/2 lb beef sirloin, marinated with Beef marinade, cooked and cut into thin strips
- 4 oz spring mix • 2 pickling cucumbers, cut julienne
- 2 leafs of red cabbage, cut julienne • 2 cups cooked short grain rice

Beef marinade
- 1 tbsp soy sauce • 1 tbsp brown sugar • 1 tsp sesame oil
- 1/2 tsp minced garlic • 1/2 tsp minced green onion

Bibim sauce
- 1+1/2 tbsp gochujang(Korean hot pepper paste) • 1 tbsp sugar
- 1 tbsp vinegar • 1 tsp sesame oil • 1 tsp toasted sesame seeds
- 1/2 tsp minced garlic • 1/2 tsp minced green onion

Mix together ingredients for Bibim Sauce and set aside.

Using a high-sided circular food mold, about 3 inches in diameter, place about 1 cup of the cooked rice inside and pack lightly. Place half of the beef on top of the rice pushing down slightly. Add half of the spring mix on top of the beef creating a "layer" on top. Then add the cucumbers and then the cabbage in a similar manner, creating a small tower with vegetable and meat layers. After all of the vegetables and meat have been layered on top of the rice, remove the mold. Repeat with the rest of the rice, meat, and vegetables, creating two towers.

Serve each tower with Bibim sauce on the side so that each person can mix together the rice, meat, and vegetables with as much sauce as she desires.

• 쇠고기 250g, 양념하여 구워서 가늘게 채 썬다. • 샐러드용 어린상추 4온스 (스프링믹스) • 오이 1개, 가늘게 채 썬다. • 적양배추잎 2장, 채 썬다. • 밥 2공기 쇠고기 양념 • 간장 1큰술 • 흑설탕 1큰술 • 참기름 1작은술 • 다진 마늘 1/2작은술 • 다진 파 1/2작은술 비빔소스 • 고추장 1+1/2큰술 • 설탕 1큰술 • 식초 1큰술 • 다진 마늘 1/2큰술 • 다진 파 1/2큰술 • 볶은 깨 1작은술 • 참기름 1작은술

다 쓴 통조림 통의 위아래 부분을 잘라내고 깨끗이 씻어 원형틀을 만든다. 원형틀 속에 밥 1컵을 넣고 누른 후 그 위에 불고기, 스프링믹스, 오이채, 적양배추채를 차례로 쌓아 살짝 눌러 빼낸 후 비빔소스와 함께 낸다. 비빔소스는 오이를 잘라 속을 판 후 그 속에 담아내면 좋다.

rice mixed with beef and vegetables 전통비빔밥 Jeontong Bibimbap

Jeontong Bibimbap is what you call the "traditional" form of bibimbap. If you order bibimbap in a Korean restaurant, this is most likely what you would be served. This is also the most popular Korean dish amongst my non-Korean friends. A fried egg and chopped meat are common additions.

- 1/3 lb beef tenderloin, cut into thin strips about 2 inches long
- 3 dried shitake mushrooms, soaked in the warm water
  to reconstitute for 30 minutes, stems discarded and cut into thin strips

Beef and mushroom marinade

- 1 tbsp soy sauce • 1 tbsp brown sugar
- 1 tsp sesame oil • 1/2 tsp minced garlic
- 1/2 tsp minced green onion

- 1 cup bracken, soaked in water and drained

Seasoning for bracken

- 1 tbsp sesame oil • 1/4 tsp salt • 1 tsp soy sauce
- 1 tsp chopped green onion
- 1/2 tsp minced garlic • 1 tsp toasted sesame seeds

- 1 cup soybean sprouts, rinsed with roots trimmed

Seasoning for soybean sprouts

- 1/2 tsp salt • 1 tsp sesame oil • 1 tsp chopped green onion
- 1/2 tsp minced garlic • 1 tsp toasted sesame seeds

- 1 cup shredded bellflower roots

Seasoning for bellflower roots

- 1/4 tsp salt • 1 tsp sesame oil • 1 tsp chopped green onion
- 1/2 tsp minced garlic • 1 tsp toasted sesame seeds

- 2 pickling cucumbers, halved lengthwise and then thinly sliced
- 1/2 carrot, peeled and cut into thin strips
- Salt • Vegetable oil • Sesame oil

• 2 eggs, cooked sunny side up • 2 cups cooked short grain rice

• daikon radish spouts for garnish (optional)

Bibim sauce

• 1+1/2 tbsp gochujang • 1 tbsp sugar • 1 tbsp vinegar

• 1 tsp sesame oil • 1 tsp toasted sesame seeds • 1/2 tsp minced garlic

• 1/2 tsp green onion, minced

Mix together ingredients for Bibim sauce and set aside.

Mix together ingredients for marinade, pour over the beef and mushrooms and set aside. Heat 1 tablespoon of oil in a frying pan and cook beef over high heat until evenly browned, about 3 minutes. Remove from pan, add mushrooms and cook for 2 minutes.

Remove the tough ends of the bracken and cut the remainder into 2 inch lengths.

Mix with seasonings and sauté over high heat in the frying pan for 5 minutes.

Scald the soybean sprouts in 1/2 cup boiling salted water, drain, and mix them with seasonings. Mix shredded bellflower roots with seasonings and sauté in the frying pan until tender for about 3 minutes.

Sprinkle sliced cucumbers with salt and let sit until the slices become soft, then squeeze out resulting moisture. Cook in 1 tablespoon sesame oil in a frying pan over high heat for 2 minutes and cool. Sauté shredded carrots in vegetable oil until softened and sprinkle with a little salt to taste.

To serve

Put cooked rice in a large bowl and arrange the other ingredients over the rice, placing the egg over the top after all the other ingredients have been arranged. Serve with the Bibim sauce. Mix with sauce to eat.

• 쇠고기 안심 150g, 5cm 길이로 채 썬다. • 말린 표고버섯 3개, 불려 채 썬다. 고기 버섯 양념장 • 간장 1큰술 • 흑설탕 1큰술 • 참기름 1 작은술 • 다진 마늘 1/2작은술 • 다진 파 1/2작은술 | • 불린 고사리 1컵 고사리 양념 • 참기름 1큰술 • 소금 1/4작은술 • 간장 1작은술 • 다 진 파 1작은술 • 다진 마늘 1/2작은술 • 볶은 깨 1작은술 | • 콩나물 1컵, 꼬리를 따고 다듬어 데쳐놓는다. 콩나물 양념 • 소금 1/2작은술 • 참기름 1큰술 • 다진 파 1작은술 • 다진 마늘 1/2작은술 • 볶은 깨 1작은술 | • 도라지 1컵, 소금에 문질러 씻어서 잘게 찢어놓는다. 도라 지 양념 • 소금 1/4작은술 • 참기름 1작은술 • 다진 파 1작은술 • 다진 마늘 1/2작은술 • 볶은 깨 1작은술 | • 오이 1개, 반으로 갈라 얇게 썰 어둔다. • 당근 1/2개, 껍질을 벗겨 채 썬다. • 소금 조금 • 식용유 적당량 • 참기름 적당량 | • 달걀 2개 반숙으로 부쳐둔다. • 밥 2컵 • 무순 한줌 (장식용) | 비빔소스 • 고추장 2큰술 • 설탕 1큰술 • 식초 2큰술 • 다진 마늘 1작은술 • 다진 파 1작은술 • 볶은 깨 1작은술 • 참기름 1큰술

쇠고기와 버섯에 준비해둔 양념을 넣어 각각 버무려 달궈진 프라이팬에 기름을 두르고 따로 볶아낸다. 고사리의 딱딱한 끝부분을 잘라낸 후 5cm 길이로 자르고 고사리양념을 넣어 볶는다. 데쳐둔 콩나물에 양념을 넣어 무친다. 준비해둔 도라지에 양념을 넣어 무친 후 달궈진 팬에 3분 정도 부드러워질 때까지 볶아낸다. 썰어둔 오이에 소금을 뿌려 살짝 절인 후 물기를 짜고 달궈진 팬에 참기름 1큰술을 두르고 2분 정도 볶는다. 썰어놓은 당근도 달궈진 팬에 식용유를 두르고 살짝 볶은 후 소금으로 간해놓는다. 준비한 그릇에 밥을 담고 준비한 고기, 버섯, 야채들, 부친 달걀을 놓고 비빔소스를 곁들여낸다.
❖ 도라지는 소금을 넣고 주물러서 씻어야 쓴맛을 제거할 수 있다.

rice with tofu and vegetables

두부야채비빔밥 Dubu Yachae Bibimbap

This bibimbap is a great vegetarian dish, something that would usually be refused in my home growing up, as we are a meat-loving family. While I still love meat, this version of bibimbap has quickly become something of a family favorite. It is a delicious way to get in my daily vegetables and with this preparation, I don't even miss the meat.

• 1/2 lb firm tofu, sliced into 1/2 inch slices

• 1 cup soybean sprouts, rinsed with roots trimmed

Seasoning for soybean sprouts

• 1/2 tsp salt • 1 tsp sesame oil • 1 tsp chopped green onion

• 1/2 tsp minced garlic • 1 tsp toasted sesame seeds

• 2 pickling cucumbers, halved lengthwise and then thinly sliced

• 2 Japanese eggplants, halved lengthwise and then thinly sliced

• 2 zucchini, halved lengthwise and then thinly sliced

• 1/2 of a carrot, peeled and cut into thin strips • Salt • Vegetable oil
• Sesame oil • 2 eggs, separated • 2 cups cooked short grain rice

Optional ingredients

• Parsley and shredded seaweed for garnish

Bibim sauce

• 1+1/2 tbsp gochujang (Korean hot pepper paste) • 1 tbsp sugar

• 1 tbsp vinegar • 1 tsp sesame oil • 1 tsp toasted sesame seed

• 1/2 tsp minced garlic • 1/2 tsp minced green onion

Mix together ingredients for Bibim Sauce and set aside.

Soak 1 paper towel in a small amount of oil and lightly oil frying pan.

Fry egg white and yolk separately, tilting pan to create a pancake.

Remove from pan and slice thinly to make egg jidan (thinly fried egg used for garnish).

Heat frying pan and add a spoonful of vegetable oil. Add tofu and pan fry both sides over medium high heat until tofu turns brown. Cut each piece of tofu into thin strips.

Scald the soybean sprouts in 1/2 cup boiling salted water, drain and mix them with Soybean Seasoning.

Sprinkle cucumbers, zucchini, and eggplant with salt and let sit until the slices become soft, and then squeeze out resulting moisture. Cook each vegetable separately in about 1 tablespoon sesame oil over high heat in a large frying pan for 2 minutes and cool. Add about 1/2 teaspoon of salt to each type of vegetable while cooking to taste. Sauté shredded carrots in vegetable oil until softened and sprinkle with a little salt to taste.

To serve

Put cooked rice in a large bowl and arrange the other ingredients over the rice, garnishing with the egg. Serve with the Bibim sauce. Mix with sauce to eat.

• 두부 1모, 1cm 두께로 썬다. • 콩나물 1컵, 꼬리를 다듬어둔다 콩나물 양념 • 소금 1/2작은술 • 참기름 1작은술 • 다진 파 1작은술 • 다진 마늘 1/2작은술 • 볶은 깨 1작은술 • 오이 1개, 길이로 반 갈라 얇게 썬다. • 가지 1개, 길이로 반 갈라 얇게 썬다. • 호박 1개, 길이로 반 갈라 얇게 썬다. • 당근 1/2개, 껍질을 벗긴 후 채 썰어둔다. • 소금 2작은술 • 식용유 1큰술 • 참기름 3큰술 • 달걀 2개 • 밥 2컵 • 선택재료: 파슬리 또는 채 썬 김 비빔소스 재료 • 고추장 2큰술 • 설탕 1큰술 • 식초 2큰술 • 다진 마늘 1작은술 • 다진 파 1큰술 • 볶은 깨 1작은술 • 참기름 1큰술 • 비빔소스 재료를 잘 섞어둔다.

달걀을 흰자와 노른자로 나누어 따로 풀어놓는다. 종이타월에 기름을 묻혀 팬에 바른 후 약불에서 흰자, 노른자 지단을 따로 부쳐 가늘게 채 썰어둔다. 달군 팬에 기름을 두르고 썰어놓은 두부를 앞뒤로 노릇하게 부쳐내어 채 썰어둔다. 냄비에 소금을 풀은 물 1/2컵과 콩나물을 넣고 뚜껑을 덮고 데쳐서 건져내 준비한 양념을 넣고 무쳐둔다. 썰어놓은 오이, 호박, 가지에 각각 소금을 뿌려 살짝 절여 물기를 짜고, 팬을 달군 후 각각 참기름 1큰술씩을 두르고 약 2분간 볶아낸다. 달군 팬에 식용유 1큰술을 두르고 채 썰어놓은 당근을 볶아 소금으로 간한다. 그릇에 밥 1컵을 담고 그 위에 볶아놓은 재료들을 골고루 담아 비빔소스와 함께 낸다.

chicken and rice porridge 닭죽 Dak Juk

There is nothing I like better for breakfast than a steaming hot bowl of my mother's Dak Juk. There are many, many different kinds of porridge in Korea. But Dak Juk is by far my favorite. In fact, in Korea there are restaurants devoted solely to porridge. The creamy rice mixes well with the tender pieces of chicken, while the sharp spiciness of the garlic and mellower green onion cuts the starchiness of the porridge perfectly. I like to add lots of freshly ground pepper right before eating to make the Dak Juk even more spicy. Whatever way you eat it, you won't find anything more satisfying on a winter's day or when you are feeling sick.

- 1 lb chicken breast with bone • 8 cups water • 1 clove garlic
- 1 green onion • 1 tsp salt • 1 tsp sesame oil
- 1 cup Korean short grain rice, wash a few times and soak the rice for 2 hours (Drain right before using for the porridge.)
- 1/2 pack enoki mushrooms, cut into 1/2 inch pieces
- 2 chopped green onions • 1 beaten egg

Boil the water in a large pot over high heat. Add green onion, garlic and chicken breast.

Boil for about 30 minutes. When chicken is tender, take out and tear meat into little pieces. Mix chicken pieces with salt and sesame oil to taste. Add soaked rice to the boiling chicken broth and continue to boil over high heat. Occasionally stir rice to keep it from sticking to the pot. Continue to boil until rice is fully cooked and soft, about 15~20 minutes. Then add seasoned chicken, enoki mushrooms, and chopped green onion to the porridge. Continue cooking for about 3 more minutes. Add beaten egg stirring well. Serve hot.

• 닭가슴살 (뼈 포함) 450g • 물 8컵 • 마늘 1쪽 • 파 1뿌리, 5cm 길이로 썰어둔다. • 소금 1작은술 • 참기름 1작은술 • 불린 쌀 1컵 • 파 2뿌리, 잘게 송송 썬다. • 달걀 1개, 풀어놓는다.

큰 냄비에 물을 넣고 끓으면 닭과 썰어둔 파, 마늘 1쪽을 넣고 센불에서 30분 정도 끓인다. 닭이 다 무르면 꺼내어 고기를 잘게 뜯어 소금과 참기름으로 밑간을 해놓는다. 국물에 불려놓은 쌀을 놓고 눋지 않게 저으면서 20분 정도 끓이다가 쌀이 다 익어 퍼지면 밑간한 닭가슴살, 잘게 썬 파를 넣고 3분 정도 더 끓인다. 불을 끄기 직전에 풀어놓은 달걀을 넣고 저어 그릇에 담아낸다.

vegetable beef porridge

야채고기죽 Yachae Gogi Juk

This porridge is made with vegetables and ground beef, and is enjoyed by both adults and children. It is also a good option for homemade baby food. Whenever I was feeling sick, my mom made this along with chicken soup. It is definitely food for the soul.

- 1/4 lb ground beef
- 1 cup Korean short grain rice, washed and soaked for about 2 hours, draining right before use
- 8 cups water • 1 tbsp sesame oil • 1 medium potato, peeled and chopped
- 1/2 carrot peeled, chopped • 1/2 onion peeled, chopped

Sauté the ground beef and rice for 3 minutes with sesame oil in a heavy frying pan, stirring continuously. Add the water and bring to a boil. Lower the heat to medium and simmer until rice is soft, about 20 minutes. Add prepared vegetables and continue to cook for 10 more minutes. Salt to taste and serve.

• 다진 쇠고기 125g • 불린 쌀 1컵 • 물 8컵 • 참기름 1큰술 • 감자 1개, 껍질 벗기고 잘게 썰어놓는다. • 당근 1/2개, 껍질 벗기고 잘게 썰어 놓는다. • 양파 1/2개, 껍질 벗기고 잘게 썰어놓는다.

달궈진 두꺼운 냄비에 참기름을 두르고 다진 소고기와 쌀을 넣어 저으면서 볶은 다음 물을 붓고 중불에서 눋지 않게 저으면서 20분 정도 끓인다. 쌀이 익어 푹 퍼지면 준비해 놓은 야채를 넣고 약 10분 정도 더 끓여낸다.

rice porridge with abalone

전복죽 Jeonbok Juk

Jeonbok Juk is a savory rice porridge cooked with minced abalone. Abalone is great in the summer. This is often served to people with weaker immune systems like children or the sick because of the high nutritional content.

- 1 cup Korean short grain rice, washed a few times and soaked for 2 hours
- 1/2 lb fresh abalone, cleaned and thinly sliced
- 1 tbsp sesame oil • 4 cups water • 1/2 tsp salt
- 1/2 pack enoki mushrooms, cut into 1/2 inch pieces (optional)
- 2 chopped green onions • 2 beaten eggs

Heat the sesame oil in a thick bottomed pot, and sauté the abalone slices for about 3 minutes over high heat. Add the drained rice and sauté for 2 more minutes. Add the water and bring to a boil. Lower the heat to medium and simmer until rice is soft, about 20 minutes, stirring occasionally. Add enoki mushrooms, green onions and beaten eggs. Stir and continue to cook for 2 more minutes. Salt to taste and serve.

• 불린 쌀 1컵 • 전복 250g, 깨끗이 씻어 잘게 썰어놓는다. • 참기름 1큰술 • 물 4컵 • 소금 1/2작은술 • 팽이버섯 1/2팩, 잘게 썰어놓는다. (선택) • 파 2뿌리, 다진다. • 달걀 2개, 풀어놓는다.

달궈진 두꺼운 냄비에 참기름을 두르고 전복을 넣어 3분 정도 볶는다. 전복이 익으면 불러놓은 쌀을 넣고 2분 정도 더 볶은 다음 물을 넣고 중불로 20분 정도 눈지 않게 저으면서 끓인다. 쌀이 다 퍼지면 썰어놓은 팽이버섯, 다진 파, 풀어놓은 달걀을 넣고 2분 정도 더 끓인 후 소금으로 간하여 낸다.

Korean party noodles 국수장국 Guksu Jangguk

In Korea, these noodles are traditionally served when people get married, which is why this dish is called Janchi Guksu(which literally means "party noodle"). It got this nickname because it is easy to expand the recipe to feed more people.

For Broth
- 4 oz beef, brisket • 1 clove garlic • 1 green onion, the white part only
- 6 cups water • Salt • 1 tsp light soy sauce • 1 tsp sesame oil

For Soup
- 1 cucumber or zucchini, seeded and cut into thin strips • 1 egg
- 1/2 carrot, cut into thin strips • 2 bundles somyeon noodle

Put water in a large saucepan and bring to a boil over medium heat. Add beef, garlic and green onion and boil until meat is fully cooked and tender, about 45 minutes. Add salt and light soy sauce to taste. Take out garlic, green onion, and beef. Discard garlic and green onion and shred the beef. Add sesame oil to shredded beef and salt to taste.

While the beef is cooking, sauté cucumber or zucchini in a hot oiled frying pan with a little salt to taste and set aside. Repeat process with carrot. Cook egg into a thin omelet and cut into thin strips. Cook somyeon noodles according to directions on the package and rinse with cold water, draining well.

Divide cooked noodles into bowls, garnishing with beef, cucumber or zucchini, carrot and egg. Pour hot broth over the noodles and serve.

• 소면국수 2인분 • 오이 또는 호박 1개, 씨를 빼고 채로 썬다. • 당근 1/2개, 껍질을 벗기고 채로 썬다. • 달걀 1개 국물 재료 • 쇠고기 150g • 마늘 1쪽 • 파 1토막 (흰 부분) • 물 6컵 • 소금 약간 • 국간장 1작은술 • 참기름 1작은술

냄비에 물을 넣고 끓기 시작하면 쇠고기, 마늘, 파를 넣어 고기가 푹 익을 때까지 (약 45분간) 끓여 체에 걸러, 국물만 냄비에 붓고 소금, 국간장으로 간한다. 고기는 가늘게 뜯어 소금, 참기름으로 간해둔다. 달궈진 팬에 기름을 두르고 채 썰어놓은 호박 (오이), 당근을 각각 볶아내어 소금으로 간해둔다. 달걀을 잘 풀어 얇게 지단으로 부쳐 가늘게 썰어놓는다. 소면을 삶아 찬물에 헹궈 손으로 말아 물기를 뺀 후 그릇에 담고 위에 준비해둔 고명을 얹고 국물을 부어낸다. ❖ 1. 쇠고기 일부를 채 썰어 양념하여 볶아 고명으로 얹어도 좋다. 2. 국수를 삶을 때 끓어오르면 찬물을 반 컵쯤 붓고 다시 끓여내면 국수가 쫄깃하게 삶아진다.

chilled soba noodle salad 쟁반국수 Jaengban Guksu

You can think of Jaengban Guksu as a noodle version of Bibimbap. This refreshing dish uses plenty of vegetables and fits wonderfully into the category of light summer cuisine. Although this recipe is great with all of the different kinds of vegetables, not all of them have to be used. In fact, you can throw in whatever you have on hand and it will still turn out wonderful.

• 3 oz soba noodles • 2 leaves green lettuce, thinly sliced

• 1/2 carrot, cut into thin strips • 1 cucumber, seeded, cut into thin strips

• 3 red radishes, cut into thin strips • 1/4 Asian pear, cut into thin strips

• 1 leaf of red cabbage, cut into thin strips

• 3 oz chicken breast, boiled and shredded

  (the resulting broth reserved for use in the soy dressing)

Optional ingredient

• daikon radish spouts and hard boiled eggs for garnish

Soy dressing

• 3 tbsp of Basic sauce (vinegar 5 : sugar 4 : salt 1)

• 1/4 cup chicken stock

  (For convenience, you can cook the chicken breast for the salad by boiling in water

  with green onion, garlic and celery and use the resulting liquid for the dressing.)

• 2 tbsp soy sauce • 1 tsp Asian hot mustard

• 1 chopped green onion • 1 tbsp sesame oil

• 1 tsp toasted sesame seeds

Mix all ingredients for soy dressing and set aside. Cook soba noodles according to directions on the package and rinse with cold water, draining well. Arrange all the prepared ingredients on a large serving plate and place noodles in the middle.

Garnish with daikon radish sprout. Add the dressing just before eating and mix together tableside.

• 모밀국수 2인분 • 상추 2잎 • 당근 1/2개, 채 썬다. • 오이 1개, 씨를 빼고 채 썬다. • 래디시 3개, 채 썬다. • 배 1/4개, 채 썬다. • 적양배추 잎 1장, 채 썬다. • 닭가슴살 90g, 삶아 가늘게 뜯고 국물은 소스를 만들 때 쓴다. 장식용 재료 (선택) 무순, 삶은 달걀이나 다른 야채를 사용해도 좋다. 간장소스 재료 • 베이직소스 3큰술 (식초 5 : 설탕 4 : 소금 1) • 닭육수 1/4컵 • 간장 2큰술 • 갠 겨자 1작은술 • 다진 파 1큰술 • 참기름 1큰술 • 볶은 깨 1작은술 간장소스 재료를 잘 섞어둔다.

모밀국수를 삶아 찬물에 헹궈 손으로 동그랗게 말아 물을 뺀 후 접시 중앙에 놓고 썰어놓은 재료들을 보기 좋게 돌려가며 담아 무순으로 장식하여 간장소스와 함께 낸다. 먹기 직전에 소스를 뿌려 섞어서 먹는다. ❖ 1. 위의 재료 대신 쇠고기 편육, 쑥갓, 맵지 않은 양파, 브로콜리, 버섯 등을 넣어도 좋다. 2. 닭고기를 삶을 때 파, 마늘, 셀러리를 넣으면 냄새를 없앨 수 있다.

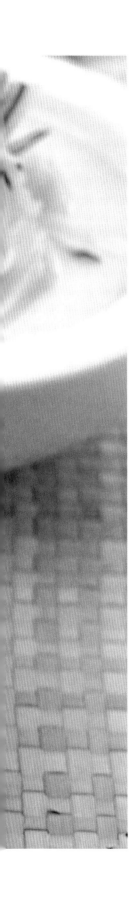

chilled noodles in soy milk 콩국수 Kong Guksu

Kong Guksu is a popular summer dish served in a chilled soy milk. Usually the noodles are homemade, but to save time, my mother buys pre-made fresh noodles at the Korean grocery store, most often found in the freezer section. The toasted sesame seeds are optional, but they add an appealing nuttiness to the dish. So, I don't recommend that you skip them.

• 1 cup dried soy beans • 1 tbsp toasted sesame seeds • 1 tsp salt

• 15 cups water • 1/2 cucumber, cut into thin strips

• 5 red radishes, cut into thin strips • 4 bundles fresh noodles or soba noodles

Wash beans and soak them in cold water for 4 hours. Rinse and remove peels. Place the beans in a large pot and add enough water to cover the beans and bring to a boil. Add 1/2 cup of cold water, and boil 5 more minutes. Remove beans from heat, rinse with cold water, then drain. In a blender, puree the beans and toasted sesame seeds with the 15 cups of water until liquefied. Strain the liquid through fine mesh strainer. Add salt to taste. Refrigerate the soy milk until ready to use.

Cook noodles according to directions on the package and rinse with cold water several times, draining well. Portion the noodles into 4 large bowls and garnish with cucumber and radish. Pour the chilled soy milk over the noodles. Serve cold.

◦ 흰콩 1컵 ◦ 볶은 깨 1큰술 ◦ 소금 1작은술 ◦ 물 15컵 ◦ 오이 1개, 채로 썬다. ◦ 래디시 5개, 채로 썬다. ◦ 칼국수용 국수 또는 모밀국수 4인분

콩을 물에 약 4시간 정도 충분히 불린 다음 깨끗이 씻어 물에 뜨는 콩껍질을 제거한다. 냄비에 넣고 물을 부은 후 뚜껑을 덮고 끓여, 끓어오르면 뚜껑을 열고 찬물 반 컵을 넣어 다시 5분 정도 더 끓인 후 찬물에 씻어 껍질을 벗긴다. 볶은 깨와 함께 블렌더에 넣어 곱게 갈아 체에 내린 후 소금간하여 차게 둔다. 먹기 직전 국수를 삶아 냉수에 헹구어 동그랗게 말아 물기를 뺀 후 그릇에 담고 콩국물을 부은 후 오이와 래디시를 얹어낸다.

chilled noodle soup 냉면 Naengmyeon

Naengmyeon literally means "cold noodle". Ironically, this chilled dish was a traditional winter time dish. When warm weather rolls around, you will find my mom eating it several times a week. In fact, when most of us are complaining about eating the same thing every day, she will make us something else for dinner and eat Nangmyeon all by herself. I certainly understand her attachment to this dish. It just tastes so good in the summer. It's also great because you can make a lot ahead of time and keep the ingredients in the refrigerator so that making dinner is quick and easy and you won't have to slave over the stove.

For beef stock
- 1/2 lb beef brisket or shank • 1/2 lb pork loin • 1/2 lb chicken breast
- 2 cloves thinly sliced garlic • 1 green onion, white part only
- 1 inch thick slice of daikon radish • 3 inch square dried kelp (kombu), washed
- 10 cups water • 2 teaspoons salt • 1 teaspoon light soy sauce

For noodle soup

- 1 (24 oz) package Korean buckwheat noodles
- 2 small pickling cucumbers, sliced into thin strips
- 8 oz daikon radish, cut into thin strips • 2 hard-boiled eggs, quartered lengthwise
- 1 Asian pear, peeled, cored and thinly sliced • 1 tsp hot chili pepper powder
- 7 tbsp Basic sauce (vinegar 5 : sugar 4 : salt 1)
- Asian hot mustard and vinegar (optional)

Prepare the daikon radish by marinating with 4 tablespoons of Basic sauce and hot chili pepper powder. Marinate sliced cucumber with the remaining 3 tablespoons of Basic sauce.

Soak the meat for the stock in cold water for 30 minutes, and drain. Place meat, kelp, daikon radish, garlic and green onion in a large pot, add the 10 cups of water and bring to a boil. Reduce heat and simmer for 1 hour, then strain the liquid through cheesecloth or a very fine mesh strainer. Slice the boiled beef into thin slices. Salt and soy sauce the broth to taste. Keep meat and stock in the refrigerator.

Cook buckwheat noodles according to directions on the package and rinse with cold water, draining well and separate the noodles into 4 portions.

Put the noodles into 4 large bowls and garnish with cucumber, radish, meat slices, pear slices and hard boiled egg. Pour the chilled soup over the noodles. Serve with Asian hot mustard and vinegar, if desired.

• 냉면국수 4인분 • 오이 1개, 반달모양으로 저며 썬다. • 무 200g, 얇고 길게 썬다. • 삶은 달걀 2개, 길게 4등분한다. • 배 1/3개, 씨를 빼고 얇게 썬다. • 고춧가루 1작은술 • 베이직소스 7큰술 (식초 5 : 설탕 4 : 소금 1) • 갠 겨자, 식초 (선택) 육수재료 • 쇠고기(양지나 사태) 200g • 돼지(등심) 200g • 닭가슴살 200g • 마늘 2쪽, 얇게 저민다. • 파 (흰 부분) 1도막 • 무 2cm 크기 1도막 • 다시마 사방 10cm 1장 • 물 10컵 • 소금 2작은술 • 국간장 1작은술

얇게 썰어둔 무에 베이직소스 4큰술과 고춧가루를 넣고 무쳐둔다. 오이는 베이직소스 3큰술을 넣어 절여둔다. 쇠고기를 30분간 담가 핏물을 빼고 나서 큰 냄비에 넣고 돼지고기, 닭가슴살, 다시마, 무, 마늘, 파, 물 10컵을 넣어 센불에서 거품을 걷어내면서 끓인다. 보글보글 끓기 시작하면 불을 줄여 1시간 정도 더 끓인다. 면보나 체에 국물을 걸러 소금과 간장으로 간하여 차게 식혀놓는다. 걸러낸 야채와 다시마는 버리고 건져낸 고기는 얇게 썰어 편육으로 준비해둔다. 냉면 국수를 쫄깃하게 삶아 찬물에 깨끗이 헹구어 동그랗게 말아 물기를 뺀다. 냉면그릇에 국수를 담고 차게 식힌 육수를 부은 후 그 위에 준비해둔 편육, 오이, 무, 배, 삶은 달걀을 얹어낸다. ❖ 1. 냉면 국수는 골고루 익도록 젓가락으로 저으면서 삶는다. 2. 물이 끓어서 넘치려고 할 때 찬물을 반 컵 정도 부으면 면이 더 쫄깃해진다. 3. 국물에 동치미 국물이나 열무김치 국물을 섞어내도 좋다.

Soba 메밀국수 Memil Guksu

Soba Sauce is a Japanese creation that has been adopted for Korean use. It makes an easy and refreshing lunch and it is extremely versatile because so many things can be added to it along with the soba noodles. The dish can be served either chilled with a dipping sauce, or in hot broth as a noodle soup.

• 4 bundles soba noodles • 1 sheet dried seaweed, shredded
• 1 inch size daikon radish, minced • 4 tbsp chopped green onion
• Prepared wasabi

Soba sauce
• 4 cups water • 4 inch square of kombu • 1/2 cup bonito flakes
• 1/4 cup sugar • 1/2 cup soy sauce
• 1/4 cup Japanese cooking wine or mirin

Wipe down kombu with dry paper towel and soak it in the water in a medium saucepan for about 10 minutes. Bring water to a boil and then turn off the heat. Add bonito flakes and leave for 5 minutes. Strain the liquid and put it back into the pot, adding the mirin, sugar, and soy sauce. Boil 5 minutes. Can be served cold.

Cook soba noodles according to directions on the package and rinse with cold water, draining well.

Divide cooked soba noodles on a plate, Pour soba sauce in a small bowl and serve with chopped green onion, shredded seaweed, minced daikon radish and wasabi.

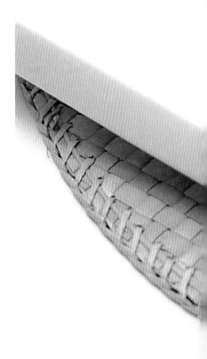

• 메밀국수 4인분 • 김 1장, 채로 썬다. • 와사비 약간 • 무 1도막(3cm), 강판에 갈아놓는다. • 실파 2뿌리 소스 재료 • 물 4컵 • 다시마 1장 (사방 10cm) • 가쓰오부시(가다랑어포) 1/2컵 • 설탕 1/4컵 • 간장 1/2컵 • 맛술 1/4컵

다시마를 마른 수건으로 깨끗이 닦아 냄비에 물과 같이 넣고 약 10분간 끓이다 거품이 나면 불을 끄고 가쓰오부시(가다랑어포)를 넣어 5분 정도 두었다가 체에 거른다. 냄비에 가쓰오부시 우린 물과 간장, 설탕, 맛술을 넣어 끓인다. 강판에 갈아놓은 무의 물기를 짜두고, 실파는 송송 썰어둔다. 큰 냄비에 물을 넣고 끓으면 소금을 조금 넣고 면을 넣어 젓다 끓어오르면 찬물을 반 컵 정도 부어 약 5분간 더 끓인다. 삶아진 국수를 찬물에 헹궈 사리를 만들어 물기를 빼고 접시나 메밀국수 판에 담아 소스와 무 간 것, 실파, 김, 와사비 등을 곁들여낸다. ❖ 1. 메밀국수 대신 소면이나 녹차국수 등 다른 면을 사용해도 좋다. 2. 소스에 얼음을 넣어 차게 먹으면 맛이 특별하다.

Kimchi

white kimchi 백김치 Baek Kimchi

Baek Kimchi is the same as traditional napa cabbage kimchee minus the hot red peppers. It's a milder version that has a refreshing taste. It is rich in vitamins and known for improving the health of your intestines as well as having some anti-bacterial, anti-virus, and anti-cancer properties. In particular, North Korea has the custom of having noodles or steamed rice in white kimchi soup on cold winter nights.

• 1 napa cabbage (about 2 lbs) • 1 green onion, cut into diagonal slices
• 1/2 of a large daikon radish, julienned • 1 carrot, peeled and julienned
• 1/2 of an apple, julienned • 1/2 cup sea salt • 3 cups water
• 1 tsp ginger juice • 1 tbsp minced garlic • 2 tbsp fish sauce • 1 tbsp sugar

Quarter the cabbage lengthwise. Soak cabbage in salt water for about 6 hours and rinse them in cold water, draining well. Place radishes, carrot and apple in a large bowl and add ginger juice, green onion, minced garlic, salt, sugar, and fish sauce and mix well. Pack the radish mixture between each leaf of cabbage.

Pack cabbages into a jar. Pour water into the mixing bowl and swirl around to get the remnants of spices. Pour water from mixing bowl over the cabbage into the jar and seal tightly. Keep jar at room temperature for 3 days to allow the kimchi to ferment. After 3 days, store the kimchi in a refrigerator.

• 배추 1통 (큰 것) • 파 1뿌리, 채 썬다. • 무 (큰 것) 1/2개, 채 썬다. • 당근 1개, 채 썬다. • 사과 1/2개, 채 썬다. • 바다소금 1/2컵 • 물 3컵 • 생강즙 1작은술 • 다진 마늘 1큰술 • 맬치액젓 2큰술 • 설탕 1큰술

소금을 물에 풀어 4등분한 배추를 담가 6시간 정도 절여 물에 깨끗이 헹구어 물기를 빼 둔다. 큰 그릇에 채 썰어둔 무, 당근, 사과와 준비해둔 나머지 양념들을 넣고 잘 섞어 배춧잎 켜켜이 속을 넣는다. 속을 넣은 배추를 잘 오므려 항아리에 넣고 남은 양념들을 물로 부셔 국물을 만들어 간을 보아 항아리에 붓고 뚜껑을 꼭 덮어 실온에 두어 3일 정도 익힌다. 익은 후 냉장보관한다.

diced radish kimchi 깍두기 Kkakdugi

Kkakdugi is made of bite-sized cubes of white radish. This is my brother's favorite type of kimchi. While there are numerous ways to make this type of kimchi, over the years my mother found this to be the best way to cosistently get the "right" taste. She simplified the process so that I could learn how to make kimchi and it's almost impossible to mess up.

- 1 large Daikon radish (about 2 lbs) • 2 tbsp ground red pepper
- 2 cloves minced garlic • 1 tsp ginger juice
- 2 green onions, cut into diagonal slices • 1 tbsp sugar
- 1 tbsp salt • 1 tbsp fish sauce

Pare radish and cut into 2cm cubes. Place cubes in a large bowl and sprinkle salt and sugar over the pieces. Let sit until radish is softened, about 1 hour. Then drain and reserve water.

Add red pepper and mix thoroughly. Then add ginger juice, green onion, minced garlic, and fish sauce and mix until coated well. If you are mixing by hand, you may want to wear protective gloves, as the red pepper tends to stain.

Pack radish cubes into a jar. Pour reserved water into the mixing bowl and swirl around to get the remnants of red pepper and spices. Pour water from mixing bowl over the radish into the jar and seal tightly. Keep jar at room temperature for 3 days to allow the kimchi to ferment. After 3 days, store the kimchi in the refrigerator.

Note

The easiest way to get ginger juice is to grate ginger root finely and squeeze the grated ginger over a small bowl.

• 무 (큰 것) 1개 • 고춧가루 2큰술 • 다진 마늘 2작은술 • 생강즙 1작은술 • 파 2뿌리, 채 썰어둔다. • 설탕 1큰술 • 소금 1큰술 • 멸치액젓 1큰술

무를 다듬어 2cm 크기로 깍둑썰기 하여 소금과 설탕을 뿌려 1시간 정도 절여둔다. 무가 다 절여지면 건져내고 국물은 따로 둔다. 건져낸 무에 고춧가루를 넣고 잘 섞어 고춧물을 들인 후 준비해둔 양념들을 넣어 버무려 병에 넣는다. 그릇에 무 절인 국물을 부어 남은 양념을 가신 후, 그 국물로 간을 맞추며 국물을 부어 실온에서 3일 정도 익힌다. 익은 깍두기는 냉장고에 넣어 보관한다. ❖ 생강즙을 만들 때, 생강을 토막 내어 얼려두었다가 필요할 때 꺼내어 전자레인지에 1분간 돌려 녹여 짜면 편리하다.

radish water kimchi

나박김치 Nabak Kimchi

Nabak Kimchi is usually made for New Year's Day meal to signify the beginning of the new year. It is symbolic of a new start, as it is made in January after you have become tired of the kimchi that you made in the fall to last you through the winter. It is popular for its cool and invigorating broth.

• 1 lb daikon radishes, cut into 1+1/2 by 1+1/2 by 1/4 inch rectangles
• 1 lb napa cabbage hearts, cut into squares • 1/2 cup sea salt
• 3 green onions, cut diagonally into 2 inch pieces
• 3 cloves garlic, peeled and finely grated • 1/3 oz ginger, peeled and finely grated
• 3 tbsp hot red pepper powder • 20 cups water • 1 tbsp hot red pepper threads
• 1 tbsp sugar • 2 oz minari (Korean watercress) cut into 2-inch pieces (optional)
• 1 empty tea bag (can be found in any Japanese grocery store)

Put hot red pepper powder in the tea bag, soak in the 20 cups of water mixed with 1/4 of a cup of the sea salt while you are preparing the rest of the ingredients. Place radish and cabbage in a large bowl. Sprinkle with 1/4 cup of the salt, toss and let stand for 30 minutes. Rinse radish and cabbage in cold water to remove salt, draining well. In another mixing bowl, combine green onion, garlic, ginger, sugar, hot red pepper threads and minari. Add radish and cabbage and toss well. Transfer the mixture to a clean glass jar. Remove hot red pepper filled tea bag from the salted water, squeeze the liquid from it and discard. Pour salted water over the radish and cabbage mixture into the glass jar. Taste and adjust the seasoning with sugar and salt if needed. Close the jar lid tight, let mature at room temperature for 2 days, and then store in the refrigerator.

• 무 1개, 사방 3cm 두께 0.5cm로 썬다. • 배추 노란 잎 1/2포기 • 바다소금 1/2컵 • 파 3뿌리, 채썬다. • 마늘 3쪽, 다진다. • 생강 1쪽, 잘게 다진다. • 고춧가루 3큰술 • 물 20컵 • 실고추 1큰술 • 설탕 1큰술 • 미나리 1/3단, 5cm 길이로 썬다. • 티백 1개

고춧가루를 티백에 넣어 물 20컵에 소금 1/4컵을 섞은 물에 담가 불려둔다. 큰 그릇에 썰어놓은 무와 배추를 넣고 소금 1/4컵을 뿌려 30분 정도 절여둔다. 무와 배추가 절여지면 물에 씻어 물기를 뺀 후 준비해둔 양념을 넣고 버무려 항아리에 담는다. 소금물에 담가둔 고춧가루 넣은 티백을 건져 물기를 짠 후 버리고 고춧물이 우러난 물에 남은 소금을 풀어 항아리에 붓는다. 이때 간이 부족하면 소금을 더 넣고 너무 짜면 물과 설탕을 조금 더 넣어 간을 맞춘다. 뚜껑을 덮고 실온에 두어 2일 정도 익힌다.

napa kimchi 통배추김치 Tongbaechu Kimchi

Napa kimchi is best described as a spicy, slightly sweet, pickled or fermented cabbage. It is the most common form of kimchi. When someone mentions "kimchi" without specifying a particular kind, this is the type of kimchi that he/she is referring to. The Korean diet is not complete without kimchi.

• 1 medium sized Napa cabbage • 1/2 cup coarse salt

• 1 green onion, cut diagonally into 1/2 inch pieces

• 1 medium sized Korean radish or Daikon radish, julienned

• 2 oz minari cut into 2 inch pieces (optional)

Marinating sauce

• 1/2 cup red pepper powder • 2 tbsp fish sauce • 1 tsp finely minced fresh ginger

• 3 tbsp minced garlic • 1/4 cup sugar • 4 tsp salt

For the sauce

Mix fish sauce and red pepper powder.
Add radish, green onion, minced garlic, sugar and salt and mix well.

Wash cabbage in cold water and drain. Cut cabbage in half lengthwise. If the cabbage is large, cut in half again. Put the cabbage in a large bowl and sprinkle the salt evenly over the cabbage and between the leaves. Add enough water to cover the cabbage and leave overnight. Rinse the cabbage under running water 2~3 times and drain well, leaving it for about 30 minutes to make sure all of the water is completely gone.

   Taking each quarter of cabbage, pack the marinating sauce between each leaf of the wilted cabbage. Tightly pack each bundle of cabbage in a container or kimchi jar. Keep at room temperature for two days, after this the kimchi must kept in the refrigerator at all times.

• 배추 1포기 • 굵은소금 1/2컵 • 파 1뿌리, 채 썬다. • 무 1개, 채 썬다. • 미나리 3줄기, 5cm 길이로 썬다. 배춧속 양념 • 고춧가루 1/2컵 • 멸치액젓 2큰술 • 다진 생강 1작은술 • 다진 마늘 3큰술 • 설탕 1/4컵 • 소금 4작은술 고춧가루에 멸치액젓을 넣어 불린 후 무, 파, 마늘, 생강, 소금, 설탕을 넣어 잘 버무린다.

배추를 길이로 4등분하여 소금을 풀어놓은 물에 6~8시간 절인다. 배추가 다 절여지면 깨끗이 헹구어 물기를 빼둔다. 배춧잎 사이사이에 버무려둔 배춧속 양념을 넣어 병에 차곡차곡 넣는다. 그릇에 묻은 양념을 물로 헹궈 소금으로 간을 맞춰 국물을 붓고 뚜껑을 덮어 실온에서 2~3일간 익힌다.

diced cucumber kimchi 오이깍두기 Oi Kkakdugi

I love Oi kakkdugi because it is an extremely easy way to prepare one of my favorite forms of cucumber kimchi. It tastes good both fresh and fermented and in a pinch, you can add some Basic sauce and eat it as a sort of spicy salad. I've been known to scoop some into a bowl and eat it plain. It is very important only to use pickling cucumbers, as other cucumbers will not be crispy after being fermented. The crispness is one of the best parts of Oi kakkdugi.

• 5 pickling cucumbers • 1 tsp salt • 1 tsp sugar

Sauce

• 1/2 carrot, peeled and shredded • 1 green onion, shredded

• 1 tsp minced garlic • 1 tsp fish sauce • 1 tsp red pepper powder

Wash cucumbers and cut off the stems and discard. Quarter each cucumber and cut in half again. Put cucumber pieces in a large bowl and sprinkle salt and sugar evenly over the top. Leave for 1 hour.

Mix all the sauce ingredients in a large bowl and add prepared cucumber. Leave it at room temperature for 24 hours, or you can eat right away. Keep refrigerated.

• 한국 오이 2개 • 소금 1작은술 • 설탕 1작은술 양념 • 당근 1/2개 • 파 1뿌리, 어슷하게 채 썬다. • 다진 마늘 1작은술 • 멸치액젓 1작은술 • 고춧가루 1작은술

오이를 씻어 양끝을 자르고 길이로 4등분하여 5cm 길이로 썬다. 큰 그릇에 썰어둔 오이를 담고 소금과 설탕을 골고루 뿌려 1시간 동안 놓아둔다. 양념을 섞어 절여둔 오이와 같이 버무려 병에 담아 실온에서 24시간 익혀 먹는다. 익지 않은 것을 먹을 때는 베이직소스를 조금 넣어 먹으면 좋다.

Dessert

red bean ice dessert 팥빙수 Pat Bingsu

Bingsu is a shaved ice dessert very popular in Korea during the summertime. There are several varieties of Bingsu, but they all contain shaved ice with fruit toppings. My mother has developed four different versions that we all enjoy at home regularly, but Bingsu topped with sweet red beans remains the one most often requested.

• 2 cups shaved ice
• 2 tbsp red beans, cooked and sweetened (can be found in any Asian grocery store)
• 1/2 cup mixed fresh fruits, chopped • 1 tbsp sweetened condensed milk
• Small sweet rice cake balls (optional) • Mint leaves for garnish

Pour shaved ice into a mound in a serving bowl. Add sweetened red beans, chopped mixed fruits, sweetened condensed milk and rice cakes. Garnish with mint leaves, and serve immediately.

You can make other varieties of Bingsu such as:

Nokcha Bingsu (Green Tea Ice Dessert), Strawberry Bingsu, Orange Bingsu

For the Nokcha Bingsu, simply add nokcha powder(matcha) to water, stir and freeze. Use the resulting ice for the shaved ice base of your Bingsu. For the Strawberry and Orange Bingsus, freeze strawberry or orange purees to use for the shaved ice.

•간 얼음 2컵 • 빙수용 팥 2큰술 • 생과일 1/2컵, 잘게 자른다. • 연유 1큰술 • 빙수용 찰떡 (선택) • 민트잎 (장식용)

간 얼음을 오목한 그릇에 담고 그 위에 달게 조린 팥, 각종 과일 썬 것, 연유, 찰떡을 얹고 민트잎으로 장식하여 낸다. 녹차빙수: 물에 가루 녹차를 섞어 얼려 갈아서 원하는 재료를 얹으면 녹차빙수가 된다. 오렌지빙수: 껍질을 벗긴 오렌지를 갈아 얼려서 빙수기에 갈아 잘게 썬 오렌지를 곁들여낸다. 딸기빙수: 딸기를 갈아 얼려서 빙수기에 갈아 잘게 썬 오렌지를 곁들여낸다.

dried persimmon with pecan

곶감쌈 Gotgam Ssam

When my mother was young, she loved Gotgam ssam as a snack, and she has definitely passed on that love to me. It is very simple and easy to make, but the combination of the nuts and the cinnamon sweet flavor of the dried persimmons is wonderful. Not only are they visually pleasing, but they are perfect as not-too-sweet desserts.

• 4 dried persimmons, stemmed and seeded • 4 whole pecans or walnuts

Take the dried persimmons and cut a slit down the middle of each. Stuff two pecans or walnuts into the slit and squeeze the persimmon to help the nuts adhere to the fruit. Cut each persimmon into 1/2 inch slices.

• 곶감 4개, 꼭지를 따고 씨를 뺀다. • 껍질을 벗긴 통피칸이나 호두 4개

씨를 뺀 곶감을 갈라 그 안에 부서지지 않은 호두나 피칸을 넣어 곶감으로 돌돌 말아두었다가 먹기 전에 1cm 두께로 썰어 접시에 예쁘게 담아낸다. ✿ 미리 만들어 랩으로 싸두었다가 필요할 때 해동하면 편리하다.

rice cakes with flower

화전 Hwajeon

Hwajeon are small sweet pancakes with flower petals of azalea, rose and more. This special Korean dessert is made mostly during holiday festivities. When flowers are not in season, you can replace flowers with dried Asian dates and parsley leaves.

• 2 cups sweet rice flour (mochiko) • 1 cup hot water
• 1/2 tsp salt • 5 dried Asian dates
• 10 parsley leaves • 1/4 cup honey • Vegetable oil for cooking

Place sweet rice flour, salt, and hot water in a large bowl. Mix together and knead well until the dough becomes soft and uniform. Tear off about 1 tablespoon of the dough and roll it out until it is a circle about 1/4 inch thick and 2.5 inches in diameter. Slice open and remove the seeds from 2 dried Asian dates, roll tightly and slice thin to make a curlicue. This will be the "flower" portion of your decoration. Pit another 3 dried Asian dates and slice into thin strips for the stems. The parsley leaves will act as the leaves.

Heat the oil in a large frying pan over medium heat. When the oil is hot, place several pieces of the dough in the frying pan and decorate with sliced dried Asian dates and parsley leaves. Cook for 3 minutes and turn and continue cooking 1 minute longer. Remove from pan, drizzle with honey and serve.

· 마른 찹쌀가루 2컵 · 뜨거운 물 1컵 · 소금 1/2작은술 · 대추 5알 · 파슬리잎 또는 쑥갓잎 10개 · 꿀 1/4컵 · 식용유

찹쌀가루와 소금을 섞어 뜨거운 물을 넣어 익반죽한다. 이때 찹쌀가루가 젖은 가루일 경우 물을 적게 넣는다. 잘 치대어 반죽이 다 되면 한술 크기로 떼어 지름 5cm 두께 0.5cm로 동글납작하게 만들어놓는다. 대추 2개는 씨를 빼고 껍질 쪽으로 돌려깎기를 하여 돌돌 말아 얇게 썰어 꽃모양을 만들고 나머지 3개는 씨를 빼고 길게 채 썰어놓는다. 팬을 중불로 달궈 기름을 두르고 만들어놓은 반죽을 대추와 파슬리 잎으로 장식하여 3분정도 두었다가 뒤집어 1분 정도 더 지져 접시에 담아 꿀을 뿌려낸다.

fried honey ginger cookies

매작과 Maejakgwa

Maejakgwa is my mother's favorite Korean dessert. I wasn't particularly fond of Maejakgwa initially because the ones I had before were store-bought, but after she made me her own, I quickly changed my mind. The minute I put one of these shiny, sticky-sweet cookies into my mouth, I was sold. The subtle ginger flavor combined with the crispy fried dough is completely addictive. Generally I feel that anything fried is delicious, and this is definitely true in the case of Maejakgwa.

- 1 cup flour • 6 tbsp water
- 1 tbsp ginger juice (the best way to obtain ginger juice is to grate ginger
  root finely and squeeze the gratings over a small bowl.
  About 1 inch of ginger root will create 1 tbsp of ginger juice.)
- 1/3 tsp salt • 2 tbsp chopped pine nuts • Vegetable oil for frying

Syrup
• 1/2 cup sugar • 1/2 cup water • 1 tbsp honey • 1 tsp ginger juice

Making the Cookies

Sift flour and salt into a mixing bowl. Add ginger juice and water and mix until a dough forms. Wrap tightly with plastic wrap and set aside for 30 minutes. Roll out dough into a sheet about 3mm thick. Cut sheet into rectangles 1 inch wide and 2 inches long. Cut a small slit lengthwise in the middle of each rectangle, leaving the ends intact. Push one end through the slit, and pull out, creating a "twist".

Fry twists in vegetable oil until they are golden brown. Dip each fried twist into the warm syrup to lightly coat and sprinkle with chopped pine nuts.

Making the Syrup

Mix together all four ingredients in a small saucepan and bring to a boil. Simmer on low heat until thickened and keep warm.

◦ 밀가루 1컵 ◦ 물 6큰술 ◦ 생강즙 1큰술 ◦ 소금 1/3작은술 ◦ 잣가루 또는 볶은 깨 2큰술 ◦ 식용유 (튀김용) 시럽 재료 ◦ 설탕 1/2컵 ◦ 물 1/2컵 ◦ 꿀 1큰술 ◦ 생강즙 1작은술

밀가루와 소금을 체에 걸러놓고 생강즙을 섞은 물로 반죽하여 랩으로 싸서 30분 정도 놓아둔다. 숙성된 반죽을 3mm 두께로 밀어 넓이 2cm 길이 5cm로 잘라놓는다. 잘라놓은 반죽 가운데에 칼집을 넣어 한끝을 가운데로 넣고 뒤집어 꼬아둔다. 냄비에 물, 생강즙, 설탕을 넣어 젓지 말고 끓여 거품이 나면 꿀을 넣어 섞고 불을 끈다. 튀김기에 기름이 뜨거워지면 준비해둔 반죽을 넣어 엷은 갈색이 될 때까지 튀겨 기름을 빼고 준비해둔 시럽에 담갔다 꺼내 잣가루나 볶은 깨를 뿌려 낸다. ❖ 1. 반죽에 녹차, 오렌지 제스트, 코코아, 호박 등을 섞어 다양하게 만들어보자. 2. 생강즙은 생강을 강판에 갈아 짜서 쓰거나, 토막을 내어 얼렸다가 전자렌지에 녹여 짜서 쓰면 편리하다. 2cm 길이의 생강을 갈면 즙이 1큰술 정도 나온다.

sweet rice with nuts and Korean dates 약식 Yaksik

You cannot miss Yaksik, a popular sweet sticky rice snack. Black Rice is often called the medicinal dessert because all of the ingredients are exceptionally good for your health. Some people like to make it with a pressure cooker, but I prefer the traditional way as it preserves the texture and tastes a lot better.

- 2 cups sweet rice, soaked in water overnight (5 hours or more)
- 1/2 cup of dried Asian dates, silvered and any seeds removed
  (Can be found in any Asian grocery store)
- 3/4 cup cooked chestnuts • 1/4 cup honey
- 1/2 cup packed dark brown sugar • 2 tbsp of sesame oil
- 1 tbsp soy sauce • Pine nuts for garnish

Drain rice and line steamer with dampened cheesecloth. Place rice in steamer and steam over medium heat for about 40 minutes, or until fully cooked and tender. Remove rice from steamer and put into a large bowl with brown sugar and honey. Mix thoroughly. Add chestnuts, dates and soy sauce and mix. Add sesame oil, and when everything is well incorporated, set aside for 20 minutes.

   Place rice mixture back into the steamer and steam again for about 30 minutes. Garnish with pine nuts and serve.

• 찹쌀 2컵, 하룻밤 불린다. • 대추 1/2컵, 씨를 빼둔다. • 밤 3/4컵 • 꿀 1/4컵 • 흑설탕 1/2컵 • 참기름 2큰술 • 간장 1큰술 • 잣 약간 (장식용)

찜통에 수건을 물에 적셔 깔고 물기를 뺀 불린 찹쌀을 넣어 40분 정도 찹쌀이 푹 익을 때까지 찐다. 큰 그릇에 찐 찹쌀, 대추, 밤, 꿀, 흑설탕, 간장을 넣어 잘 섞은 다음 참기름을 넣어 다시 한번 섞어 간이 배게 20분 정도 둔다. 잘 섞여진 찰밥을 찜통에 다시 넣고 30분 정도 더 쪄낸다. 1인분씩 동그랗게 뭉쳐 잣이나 파슬리 등으로 장식하여 낸다. ❖ 1. 밤은 한창일 때 구입하여 살짝 구워 껍데기를 간 채로 얼려두었다가 필요할 때 쓰면 좋다. 2. 대추는 빨간 빛이 진하고 윤기가 나는 중간 크기의 것이 좋다. 3. 압력솥에 만들어도 편리하지만, 찜통에 쪄내는 것이 쫄깃하고 더 맛이 좋다.

sweet rice balls 경단 Gyeongdan

When developing this recipe my mother used the Japanese rice flour typically used for mochi, which is completely dried, as opposed to the glutinous rice flour found in most Korean grocery stores. The rice flour in Korean grocery stores is found in the refrigerated section and is a bit more moist than the Japanese variety. If you choose to use the Korean variety, less water should be added when kneading the rice dough.

Dough(for 2 dozen rice balls)

• 1 cup sweet rice flour (mochiko) • 1/2 cup hot water • 1/4 tsp salt

For Syrup

• 1/4 cup sugar • 1/4 cup water • 1 tbsp ginger juice

For Topping

• 2 tbsp pine nuts, chopped • 2 tbsp toasted sesame seeds

• 1 tbsp ground cinnamon

Place sweet rice flour, salt, and hot water in a medium bowl. Mix together and knead well until the dough becomes soft and uniform. Divide the dough into 24 little balls.

In a medium pot, bring about 6 cups of water to a boil. Drop the balls into the boiling water. Once each ball comes up to the surface of the water, let it cook for 3 more minutes. As the balls finish cooking, take them out and place them in cold water and drain well.

Put the sugar, water and ginger juice into a small saucepan and bring to a boil. Dip the cooked rice balls in the syrup and roll them in the different prepared toppings.

재료 (24개) • 마른 찹쌀가루 1컵 • 뜨거운 물 1/2컵 • 소금 1/4작은술 시럽 재료 • 설탕 1/4컵 • 물 1/4컵 • 생강즙 1작은술 고물 재료 • 잣가루 2큰술 • 볶은깨 2큰술 • 계피가루 1큰술, 설탕 1큰술을 넣고 섞어놓는다.

찹쌀가루에 소금, 뜨거운 물을 넣어 반죽한다. 잘 치대어 반죽이 다 되면 24개로 나누어 동그랗게 빚어놓는다. 중간크기의 냄비에 물 6컵을 넣고 끓으면 빚어놓은 반죽을 넣어 삶아, 떠오르면 3분 정도 더 끓이다가 찬물에 헹궈 물기를 빼놓는다. 냄비에 물, 생강즙, 설탕을 넣어 젓지 말고 끓여 거품이 나면 불을 끈다. 물기를 뺀 떡을 시럽에 담갔다가 준비해놓은 잣가루, 계피가루, 볶은 깨 등에 각각 굴려낸다. ❖ 1. 찹쌀가루가 젖은 가루일 경우 물을 적게 넣는다. 2. 곱게 부순 카스텔라, 볶은 검정깨, 또는 팥을 삶아 으깨서 고물로 써도 좋다.

rice punch 식혜 Sikhye

Sikhye is made from rice and malt. Making Sikhye takes so long that my mother would start preparing it after dinner and finish up after we went to bed. I would smell Sikhye as I went to sleep and wake up excited to drink it with my breakfast. The rice and pine nut garnishes are an important part of my enjoyment of the drink, but the Sikhye tastes great on its own, too.

• 2 cup yeotgireum (malt) • 1 cup Korean short grain rice, washed and soaked

• 2 cups sugar, or to taste • 20 cups of water

• 2 tbsp pine nuts for garnish

Combine 20 cups of water and malt, mix well and let sit for about 2 hours, letting the malt soak into the water. The liquid should eventually separate into two layers. Cook rice in the rice cooker as you would usually do and set aside. Carefully pour the top part of clear malt water over the cooked rice, set the rice cooker to warm, and leave about 7 hours or until 4~5 rice grains float to the top. Take the liquid out of the rice cooker, and separate rice grains from the liquid. Wash the rice in water and drain. Boil the rice liquid in a large pot and add the sugar to taste. Let it cool and store in a refrigerator. Pour the sikhye in a small bowl and garnish with washed rice and pine nuts. Serve cold.

• 엿기름 2컵 • 쌀 1컵, 씻어서 불려놓는다. • 설탕 2컵 • 물 20컵 • 잣 2큰술

엿기름을 물 20컵에 주물러 풀어 2시간 정도 앙금이 가라앉을 때까지 둔다. 전기밥솥에 불린 쌀을 넣고 밥을 고슬고슬하게 지어, 앙금이 가라앉은 엿기름의 맑은 물만 따라 붓고 밥솥을 보온으로 놓아 약 7시간 동안 또는 밥알이 4~5알 위로 떠오르기 시작할 때까지 삭힌다. 다 삭은 밥알은 체에 걸러 찬물에 헹구어 전분기를 씻어내고, 식혜물은 냄비에 붓고 설탕을 섞어 끓인다. 이때 떠오르는 거품은 걷어내고 조금 더 끓인 후에 차게 식혀 냉장고에 두고 먹을 때 밥알 조금과 잣을 몇 알 띄워낸다.

cinnamon punch
with dried persimmon

수정과 *Sujeonggwa*

Sujeonggwa is a sweet refresher with persimmon, cinnamon, and ginger. My mother loves surprising me with Sujeonggwa when I come home for a visit. It is usually served after dinner with buttery pine nuts floating on the top as a dessert. I especially love fishing out the dried persimmons and eating them before downing the gingery concoction.

• 6 cups water • 2 cinnamon sticks

• 2 oz ginger, peeled and thinly sliced • 1/2 cup honey

• 4 dried persimmons, stemmed and seeded

• 2 whole pecans or walnuts

Put ginger and cinnamon sticks in a large pot with the water and bring to a boil. Lower heat and simmer for 30 minutes. Add honey and mix well, then strain through a fine mesh sieve. Discard ginger and cinnamon and place the mixture in the refrigerator to chill. About 1 hour before serving add 2 dried persimmons to the punch to flavor and allow the dried fruit to soften.

Take the other 2 persimmons and cut a slit down the middle of each. Stuff two pecans or walnuts into the slit and squeeze the persimmon to help the nuts adhere. Cut each into 1/2 inch slices. Pour it into dessert bowls and put one slice of persimmon in each bowl. Serve with a spoon.

• 물 6컵 • 통계피 50g • 생강 50g, 껍질을 벗기고 얇게 저민다. • 꿀 1/2컵 • 곶감 4개, 씨를 빼둔다. • 통호두 또는 피칸 2개

큰 냄비에 생강과 통계피를 넣고 끓여 물이 끓기 시작하면 불을 줄여 30분 정도 더 끓인 후 꿀을 넣어 잘 섞어 체에 받쳐 차게 식혀 냉장고에 넣어둔다. 먹기 약 1시간 전에 곶감을 국물에 넣어 맛이 우러나오게 둔다. 씨를 뺀 곶감 2개는 한끝을 갈라 그 안에 부서지지 않은 통호두나 피칸을 넣어 곶감으로 돌돌 말아 1cm 두께로 썰어 둔다. 그릇에 수정과 국물을 붓고 곶감쌈을 두어 개 띄워 내거나 불린 곶감과 잣을 띄워낸다.

Kye Kim's Modern Korean Cooking 케이 킴의 모던 한국요리

Text Copyright ⓒ Kye Seon Kim 2009
Photo Copyright ⓒ Kye Seon Kim 2009
이 책의 모든 레시피, 사진, 요리팁은 저작권법에 따라 보호를 받습니다.

초판인쇄 2009년 1월 20일 **초판발행** 2009년 1월 30일

지은이 케이 킴 **펴낸이** 김정순 **책임편집** 심선영 **디자인** 김리영
펴낸곳 (주)북하우스 퍼블리셔스 **출판등록** 1997년 9월 23일 제406-2003-055호 **주소** 121-840 서울시 마포구 서교동 395-4 선진빌딩 6층
전자메일 editor@bookhouse.co.kr **홈페이지** www.bookhouse.co.kr **전화번호** 02-3144-3123 **팩스** 02-3144-3121

ISBN 978-89-5605-317-2 13590

이 도서의 국립중앙도서관 출판도서목록(CIP)은 e-CIP 홈페이지(http://www.nl.go.kr/ecip)에서 이용하실 수 있습니다.(CIP제어번호:CIP2009000080)